Praise for
Soul and the City

"I actually started reading Marcy Heidish's *Soul and the City* on a subway train, and I must say it had exactly the effect she writes about. It gave me peace in the middle of the hurry, the rush, the loud noise of the city."

> —RICK HAMLIN, executive editor of *Guideposts* and author
> of *Finding God on the A Train*

"*Soul and the City* is a deeply inspiring call to awareness, to connection with God and with others, and ultimately to soulful worship through so many aspects of life in the city that we find mundane, undesirable, or that even often go unnoticed. Almost instantly, upon delving into its pages, you find your perspective changed."

> —SARAH ZACHARIAS DAVIS, author of *Confessions from an
> Honest Wife, Transparent,* and *The Friends We Keep*

"Marcy Heidish has compiled a rich and nuanced touring companion to rival any Michelin or Eyewitness guide—usable in any city of the world. Keep it close and you will not only find your way amidst the city's noise and rush, you will meet beauty and holiness no matter where you pause to look."

> —LEIGH MCLEROY, author of *The Beautiful Ache* and
> *The Sacred Ordinary*

Soul
AND THE
CITY

ALSO BY MARCY HEIDISH

FICTION

A Woman Called Moses

Deadline

Miracles

The Secret Annie Oakley

The Torching

Witnesses

NONFICTION

A Candle at Midnight: Keeping Vigil as a Path Through Depression

Who Cares? Simple Ways You Can Reach Out

Soul
AND THE
CITY

Finding God in the Noise and Frenzy of Life

Marcy Heidish

WATERBROOK
PRESS

SOUL AND THE CITY
PUBLISHED BY WATERBROOK PRESS
12265 Oracle Boulevard, Suite 200
Colorado Springs, Colorado 80921
A division of Random House Inc.

All Scripture quotations are taken from the King James Version.

Details in some anecdotes and stories have been changed to protect the identities of the persons involved.

ISBN 978-1-4000-7436-5

Published in the United States by WaterBrook Multnomah, an imprint of The Doubleday Publishing Group, a division of Random House Inc., New York.

WATERBROOK and its deer design logo are registered trademarks of WaterBrook Press, a division of Random House Inc.

Library of Congress Cataloging-in-Publication Data
Heidish, Marcy.
    Soul and the city : finding God in the noise and frenzy of life / Marcy Heidish. — 1st ed.
        p. cm.
    Includes bibliographical references (p. 203) and index.
    ISBN 978-1-4000-7436-5
    1. Cities and towns—Religious aspects—Christianity. 2. City dwellers—Religious life. I. Title.
    BR115.C45H44 2008
    248.409173'2—dc22
                                            2008001349

Printed in the United States of America
2008—First Edition

10 9 8 7 6 5 4 3 2 1

SPECIAL SALES
Most WaterBrook Multnomah books are available in special quantity discounts when purchased in bulk by corporations, organizations, and special interest groups. Custom imprinting or excerpting can also be done to fit special needs. For information, please e-mail SpecialMarkets@WaterBrookMultnomah.com or call 1-800-603-7051.

*In loving memory
of Rev. Thomas P. Gavigan, SJ,
mentor, guide,
teacher, model,
friend*

CONTENTS

1 Finding God in the City—*The Gateway for Seekers* 1

2 Finding God in Crowds—*The Gateway to Connection*. 9

3 Finding God in Noise—*The Gateway to Stillness* 26

4 Finding God in Haste—*The Gateway to Deliberation* 44

5 Finding God in Stress—*The Gateway to Serenity* 64

6 Finding God in Distractions—*The Gateway to Simplicity* . . . 86

7 Finding God in Chaos—*The Gateway to Peace* 101

8 Finding God in Gutters—*The Gateway to Giving* 119

9 Finding God in Aloofness—*The Gateway to Mercy* 138

10 Finding God in Isolation—*The Gateway to Community* . . . 156

11 Finding God in Emptiness—*The Gateway to Worship* 171

12 Finding God in the Concrete—*The Gateway to Gratitude* . . . 188

Notes 195

Bibliography 203

Index 211

*A city that is set on a hill
cannot be hid.*
—MATTHEW 5:14

⎯⎯⎯◌◍◌⎯⎯⎯

*Oh, what a beautiful city…
Twelve gates to the city,
Hallelujah!*
—AFRICAN AMERICAN SPIRITUAL

FINDING GOD IN THE CITY

The Gateway for Seekers

The nave's blue light bathes me. The midtown church arches over its visitors. Quietly, I stop to pray. After a few hushed moments, I become aware of a woman beside me. She hovers there, shifting from one foot to the other. Sensing some spiritual urgency, I offer my spot to her for her own prayer.

But the woman remains standing, hands on hips, and confronts me: "So. Tell." She leans closer. "I gotta know." She leans closer still. "Who does your hair?"

In an urban environment, it's easy to be distracted from our spiritual focus, even in a glorious house of worship. The traditional spiritual aids of silence, solitude, simplicity, and serenity aren't always available in a city. The pace is fast, rather than contemplative. Nature's focal points are scarce amid glass-and-concrete towers. Prayer can seem muted by traffic noise and vendors' cries. In bustling streets, it may be difficult to make time and space to practice God's presence. And yet…isn't it in the metropolis, the marketplace, the municipal magnet that we often feel the greatest need for a sense of the sacred?

Sin.

Stress.

Seduction.

Soul-lessness.

For many people, these words are synonymous with city life—and they form a time-honored viewpoint. As symbols of evil, the biblical cities of Sodom and Gomorrah live in our collective consciousness; the name of one has even entered our language. Throughout Scripture, folklore, and literature, the "big city" is often seen as a tempting nexus of vice where we stand in real danger of losing our souls. Is it any wonder that New York City is dubbed the "Big Apple," a large and luscious logo for original sin?

This image of cities lingers in the modern imagination. In Bernard Malamud's famous novel *The Natural,* the young hero, Roy Hobbs, leaves his farm and loses his innocence in Chicago, where he suffers a deep fall from grace. In the classic story *The Wizard of Oz* by L. Frank Baum, the heroine, Dorothy, sets out to find "the answer" in the fabled Emerald City. Like a pilgrim, she travels with other seekers, only to find that the Wiseman of Oz is a fraud, and the city lives up to its archetypal image of hucksterism, especially compared with Dorothy's home on a Kansas farm.

These themes stand in a long tradition of cautionary tales about the soul and the city—not just in folklore, but in the Bible. There, writes Robert C. Linthicum, "the city is depicted as both a dwelling place of God and his people and as a center for Satan and his minions. The city is one primary stage on which the drama of salvation is played out. And that is no less the case as mega-cities become the focal point for most human activity and aspirations in the world."[1]

Cities, however, are also strongly associated with the sacred. In Scripture and song, heaven itself is often portrayed as a city. Jerusalem, Rome, Mecca, Canterbury, and other earthly cities are enduring metropolitan centers dedicated to the holy.

In the Middle Ages, the great cathedrals of Europe rose in cities. For centuries, these cities have attracted pilgrims who still come to gather in reverence, from Compostela in Spain, to Canterbury in England, and of course to that crossroads of faith, Jerusalem. Modern cities attract pilgrims too: seekers of all ages, who come for change, opportunity, and—increasingly now for retirees—culture and convenience.

I've always gravitated toward cities to find inspiration from their diversity and their culture. When I first moved back to Manhattan, I thought the museums, theater, and concerts would fill my soul. The cultural life was indeed superb. Still, I found that I needed a deeper sense of inspiration in the urban landscape's busyness.

I'm not alone.

Today, cities and large towns are home to millions of people who have *not* lost their souls—and who have created beautiful, diverse houses of worship, testaments to that fact. City dwellers and urban commuters still seek the spiritual dimension, one that saturates their routines, sustains them through the demands of urban stress, and gives life a greater depth. There's a hunger for something more than externals, for something that runs as a deeper, enduring current to nourish the soul in the city.

Thomas Moore wrote: "Care of the soul is inspiring. The act of entering into the mysteries of the soul, without sentimentality or pessimism, encourages life to blossom forth according to its own designs and with its own unpredictable beauty."[2]

"In spite of everything I had, all that I had accomplished," writes physician Paul A. Wright, of Steubenville, Ohio, "I still had not achieved my ultimate goal in life: inner peace and happiness.… As my medical practice grew, so did my stress."[3]

From the Midwest to the East and West Coasts the story is the same. *New York Magazine* has run stories on urban burnout, especially among the young and wealthy, and the quest for peace of mind continues throughout all cities.

"Power, success, happiness, as the world knows them, are his who will fight for them hard enough; but peace, love, joy are only from God," writes Frederick Buechner in *The Magnificent Defeat*.[4]

We may wrestle with that admission, as Jacob wrestled with the Angel, but this is a truth that urban living can reveal to us in surprising ways.

No one observes this better than Buechner. In *The Hungering Dark,* he wrote about seeing a Fellini film, *La Dolce Vita,* in which a huge, holy statue was being carried by helicopter to Vatican City. The statue hung from a harness of the chopper and attracted laughter from the movie audience as the young pilots descended slightly to ogle some girls sunbathing on a roof. But as the helicopter approached the city, the camera zoomed in on the statue until the face of Christ filled the screen. Buechner noted that the audience in the theater fell silent. Suddenly it was "as if the face were their face somehow, their secret face that they had never seen before…or the face that they knew, if only for a moment, they belonged to."[5]

In a city, perhaps more than in any other locale, we have God's face all around us, if we look for it—not in the sky, but in the faces of others. Whether we're talking about Los Angeles or Louisville or Bakersfield or Bend, cities can show us how varied we are as human beings: varied in ethnicity, race, age, style, health. We might think the cityscape hides God, but in a unique way, a metropolis reveals God's presence through the diversity of His children, for all are created in God's image.

Our Restless Hearts

I remember when I returned to a city after living briefly in a small town. At first, I was stunned by the spread of concrete, the roar of traffic, the faster pace, the near absence of birdsong and foliage. On a busy street, I stopped someone to ask for the time and was rewarded with a smile, an answer, and a sudden sense of connection.

As I opened myself more fully to others, this sense increased. The city's very restlessness seemed shared with the crowds I joined.

"O God, you have made us for yourself, and our hearts are restless until they find their rest in you," Saint Augustine wrote in his famous *Confessions.*[6]

How well this applies to those of us who live in metropolitan areas and large towns—or who commute to them daily or weekly. Few of us can run away to a retreat house whenever we feel a spiritual need, which may be as frequent as every day. How then do we respond to our need for peace, for spiritual connection, for that something more that gives life dimension and deeper meaning? How do we find God in the contemporary city? Does the city conceal God from us or reveal Him in unexpected ways?

I've come to believe the answers are closer than we realize. Cities, despite first impressions, can and do offer us dynamic opportunities to forge, deepen, and transform our spiritual lives. Screaming sirens give us a chance for anonymous intercession. Skyscrapers, like spires and minarets, lift our eyes. A red traffic signal gives us a moment for petition or praise. And everywhere, the homeless and the broken demand our compassion.

What we once might have seen as distractions can instead be spiritual openings—"gateways," I call them, or invitations and beckonings to God's presence. Each gateway invites us into a deeper spirituality, not in spite of the city, but because of it. In a cityscape, for example, there are plentiful ways to pair prayer with social service. We're challenged to see God in the speed and stress of the urban scene but can find spiritual oases in parks, museums, concert halls, and varied houses of worship.

Cities give us a keen opportunity to integrate the spiritual life with the worldly life. The urban environment weaves together both elements in a pungent, sometimes paradoxical, blend. I realize that the Holy can come to me not only in retreat houses or church gardens but right where I am: in the midst of multitudes. I can reach out, I can worship, not only in privacy but even caught in a crush of others—on a street, on a highway, in a cityscape.

This is part of everyone's spiritual legacy, everyone's story. And when I reflect on this truth, I must admit that it comes as something of a shock to me. This is not the venue I expected for a spiritual life. But I am finding it surprising and rich.

You can too.

In the following chapters, discover with me new kinds of spiritual practice seen through an urban lens. Like the diverse nature of cities themselves, I've drawn upon a wide range of sources—from Mother Teresa of Calcutta to Frank Laubach, the evangelical missionary who developed a vast literacy program in the Philippines. Every chapter includes useful questions and ideas for measuring soulsickness in the city as well as a psalm and cures ("Stop," "Yield," and "Go") to reflect upon, discuss with others, and try on your own.

The Holy One *can* be rediscovered in the city, where we can find, in Gerard Manley Hopkins' words, a world that is "charged with the grandeur of God."[7]

⸺⸻∞⸻⸺

> *O God, thou art my God; early will I seek thee: my soul thirsteth*
> *for thee, my flesh longeth for thee in a dry and thirsty land,*
> *where no water is;*
> *To see thy power and thy glory, so as I have seen thee in the sanctuary.*
> *Because thy lovingkindness is better than life, my lips shall praise*
> *thee.*
> *Thus will I bless thee while I live: I will lift up my hands in thy*
> *name. (Psalm 63:1–4)*

CURES FOR *Soulsickness* IN THE CITY

Stop: Read and Receive

1. Am I an urban person or an urban commuter seeking a greater depth in my spiritual life?
2. What would a deepened spiritual life look like for me in the city—or passing through one?
3. What aspects of my city overpower my spiritual life?
4. Which aspects of my city enhance my relationship with God? The city's energy? diversity? cultural life? What can I celebrate and tap to feed my soul?

Yield: Reflect, Journal, or Discuss

5. When I reflect frankly, do I tend to see my city more as a version of the biblical Babylon or as the holy city of Jerusalem? How so?
6. If I see the city both ways, can I live with my ambivalence or do I need to make some changes?
7. When I seek to deepen my spirituality, do I find myself overwhelmed with the stimuli and distractions of a big city?
8. I can balance a city's many opportunities with time for God these three ways. (List three ideas.)

Go: Experience and Engage

9. Begin keeping a journal about your spiritual experiences in the city. Watch, reflect, and listen to God, yourself, and the city itself. Start today. Where did you feel a soulsickness? When did you sense God—in what circumstance? Describe what happened and how you felt about the moment.

10. Offer up to God this time of reading, reflecting, and journaling as a form of worship.
11. Write a brief prayer about your heart in the city—what you love and are grateful for, what you lack and yearn for.
12. Discern where you most need soul in the city:

    At my home because (fill in this blank)

    _____
    _____.

    At my work because (fill in this blank)

    _____
    _____.

    Where I go for entertainment and social life because (fill in this blank)

    _____
    _____.

    Where I go for groceries, services, and supplies because (fill in this blank)

    _____
    _____.

FINDING GOD IN CROWDS
The Gateway to Connection

A man is grating beets at a major intersection in midtown Manhattan.

Squatting on a tarp, he flicks his tool, showing how it shaves the sturdy purple vegetable in his hand. Crowds surge past him. Hurried people step over his wares. Traffic lights change, and another wave of pedestrians circumvents him. He reaches for a carrot as a bus screeches to a stop and disgorges its passengers. Exhaust fumes streak the air. A homeless woman gulps water from a decorative fountain, and a bicycle messenger swiftly dodges the grater of vegetables.

Near him, I stand frozen, overwhelmed by the crowds. I wonder why I ever came back to this city. Is it possible to have any kind of spiritual life here? Can I sense God's presence here? I need that; I've always needed that, even when the need was rudimentary and intensely private—and I know I'm not the only one with that thirst, that desire.

Millions of urban people seek spiritual lives that go beyond weekly gatherings for corporate worship—lives that reach beneath the urban forest to nurture the very roots of their beings. We need "to be quiet for a while, each day, in a world that prizes activity. We want to rest and reconnect with what makes us brave," writes Claudia Horwitz in *The Spiritual Activist*.[1] Whether or not we belong to a religious community, whether we even speak of spiritual need, for so many of us, "what makes us brave" is time and space for God.

How to find this in a crowd?

How to find it at a frenetic urban intersection, where the only island of peace seems to be a beet grater's tarp, spread on concrete?

That afternoon, as I stood beside him, I had a simple urge to flee to a house of worship, to find refuge in a church's lakelike light, as I did from the time I was a child. But I am no longer a child; somehow I had to discover a way to sense God in the cityscape and its crowds. I could only stand there, pinned like a moth to the corner of Lexington and Fifty-seventh, buffeted by more people, and murmur, "God, help me."

At that corner, encased in a raised metal sleeve, a construction cable stretched across the sidewalk. I watched a frail, elderly woman approach the cable with hesitation and apprehension. She paused, reaching out to me, just as I instinctively reached out to her. Our hands clasped; our eyes met. There was a small, still moment. And then she crossed over the barrier. We exchanged murmured words, and she passed on, finally lost in the crowd.

As I strained for a glimpse of her, I was reminded of Thomas Merton's words in *Conjectures of a Guilty Bystander*. To be exact, in the section called "The Vision of Louisville," Merton wrote about a transformative moment experienced in Louisville, Kentucky:

> At the corner of Fourth and Walnut, in the center of the shopping district, I was suddenly overwhelmed with the realization that I loved all these people, that they were mine and I theirs, that we could not be alien to one another, even if we were total strangers. And they were all walking around shining like the sun. It was like waking from a dream of separateness.[2]

Mark Lewis, a pastor in Secaucus, New Jersey, underscores this view: "There is a promise before us that a vision of the world and everything in it is suffused with divine light…possible for everyone." Even in city crowds, *especially*, perhaps, in city crowds, where such a vision is so needed, where the world is too much with us, where we are weary, worried, rushed, and crushed, even there "is a dazzling reality just beneath the surface and if you want, that's what you can see."[3]

For many people, a fast-moving throng seems to hum with excitement or pulse with energy. A friend says that he experiences a stronger sense of the life force on crowded city streets than anywhere else. He thrives on the human diversity and the pace that a metropolis offers.

For others, though, urban crowds mean congestion, chaos, jostling, and stress, none of which seem conducive to spirituality. Another friend says she thinks of herself "ricocheting off the elbows of strangers" as she navigates her way through big-city streets. Another likens a crowd to a herd of bison, ready to stampede.

There's even a term called "crowd-sickness," which may especially affect those with sensitive, empathetic natures: the feeling of being bombarded by too much—too many people, too much energy. Some people develop agoraphobia (literally "fear of the marketplace"), which causes anxiety or panic not only in throngs of people but in open spaces as well.

Although I don't suffer from agoraphobia, I've often found urban crowds challenging to my own spirituality. I'm a private person with a quiet life and a contemplative nature; although I've lived most of my life in large metropolitan areas, my sense of crowd stress has dissipated only recently. It happened when I took that stranger's hand and looked into her face.

God in Others

Human connection seems to be an antidote to crowd-sickness. We are created in God's image—and yet, how easy it is to lose hold of this foundational belief. Like J. Brent Bill, author of *Mind the Light*, I often forget to look for God in the faces of the urban tableau.[4] For a long time, the faces used to blur and I felt overwhelmed by the multitudes. Sometimes, I simply didn't look at individual faces. I too easily lost that sense of "otherness" and only felt the pressure to keep moving, to navigate my own path.

How much I've missed.

"When I see God shining in the facial expressions, comments, and body language of the people I see every day, I appreciate things that separate us," Bill writes. "Such seeing doesn't deny the differences, but helps me to perceive them as gifts. This then leads me further down the path where there's a possibility of my learning to love [others] in the same way God loves them and me."[5]

But what of the people in crowds who do not seem lovable to us?

In cities we see a wide variety of humanity. Few of us are beautiful; some of us are angry, aggressive, jostling, and pushing. Many are on the fringes of society, displaying individual brokenness for all to see. Some seem to have it all, the stylish and well-heeled: easier to judge or envy, perhaps, than to care for.

"You can see the beauty of Christ in each individual person, in that which is most his, most human, most personal to him," advised Thomas Merton.[6]

There is a Jewish prayer that reminds me to see God in others: "Blessed art thou, Lord our God, King of the universe, who dost vary the aspect of Thy creatures." This prayer is to be said when "seeing a person of abnormal appearance."[7] While it's difficult to say what normal is—we each have our abnormalities, our own idiosyncrasies, obvious or hidden—such prayers unite us in our diversity. Such prayers can help us amid the crowd to praise God for our differences. It's worth noting too that these prayers are not reserved only for solitude, but designed for life on the move—real, chaotic life.

The Holy Ordinary

If we attempt to be mindful of others, we can see the holy in the ordinary: a keystone of many spiritual traditions. Dorothy Day, the journalist and social activist, said, "Christ is always with us, always asking for room in our hearts.... It is...with the eyes of store clerks, factory workers and children that he gazes; with the hands of...slum dwellers and suburban housewives that he gives."[8]

But this viewpoint may be challenging to us. We don't see halos around the heads in a crowd, Day admitted. "If everyone were holy and handsome, with...neon lighting [around] them, it would be easy to see Christ in everyone."[9]

A crowd challenges us to see others with compassionate eyes. And a city multitude teaches us other disciplines as well, among them patience, respect, and tolerance. I'm constantly learning this when caught in a crush of people moving more slowly or more quickly than I am. It's so easy to grow impatient or defensive; it's not so easy to have the patience with others that God has with us. But when I bear this in mind, I find a greater peace within. I notice too how often people make way for others and respect individual space.

Paul said that in God "we live, and move, and have our being" (Acts 17:28).

How often we miss an encounter with God if we do not look for the Holy One in the people we walk among in a crowd.

I know many people who say they like to people-watch. Perhaps people-watching could take on a spiritual dimension when we're mindful of God in each person. This mindfulness takes practice and a willing heart. I fail more often than not. But I'm not alone as I try and fail and try again; the Holy One is with me. This we are each promised.

Prayer in Crowds

Several years ago I had the privilege of doing volunteer work with homeless women. I'll always remember the woman I'll call Nell, who had a kind heart, a pink plastic purse from Goodwill, and a vast memory of Scripture from her Baptist tradition. In a shelter's Bible study session, we discussed that seed of secret growth present within each of us.

"Sometimes," Nell said, "life presses me down so hard, I can't pray nohow." She paused. "That's when the little seed inside me prays for me." The Holy Spirit, she explained, was not concerned with where she was—she could be on the street or in a crowd and be in prayer at the same time. Crowds and noise didn't faze her. But even Nell felt a need for solitary prayer at times. Every day, she would say, it's important to take some moments for quiet prayer.

She didn't mean limit your prayer life to solitude and rule out those vast expanses of time when you're among others. Who, after all, can limit God or the ways God comes to us? We cannot limit where or when God's presence feels immanent, intimate, close.

"Solitude," writes Richard Foster in *Celebration of Discipline,* "is more a state of mind and heart than it is a place. There is a solitude of the heart that can be maintained at all times. Crowds, or lack of them, have little to do with this inward attentiveness.... Whether alone or among people, we always carry with us a portable sanctuary of the heart."[10]

Foster's not writing about that painful form of loneliness that comes from feeling alone in a crowd. He's describing that sense of an inner, portable sanctuary, cupped within us, not an attribute of especially holy people, but part of us all—the part that Jesus told us was like a seed growing in good soil (see Matthew 13:23).

Breath Prayer

I learned a great deal about praying in crowds from homeless women, especially Nell. She practiced prayer on the street by holding a phrase from a hymn, a song, or Scripture with her throughout the day and repeating it to herself—and to God. Sometimes, she said, the phrase was short. For example, "Lord, have mercy on me." Sometimes she would vary this phrase by praying it as intercession: "Lord, have mercy on her/him/them." Other times the phrase was longer. Nell chose a new phrase every morning and sometimes, when sorely pressed, used a different one for morning, afternoon, and evening. Often she suited her phrase to her spiritual need: "Lord, get me through," or, "Dear God, hold me close."

Without realizing it, Nell was following an ancient tradition from the Eastern Orthodox Church: a devotional expression called "aspiratory prayer" or "breath prayer": a prayer that can be said (aloud or silently) in one breath. In this tradition, the Psalter is often the source of such prayers. A couple of phrases could evoke for Nell a whole psalm, remembered and recited silently. "I fear no evil" and "for Thou art with me" brought back the entire Twenty-third Psalm, with its message of God's comfort and enduring presence.

Whether her inspiration was from the Psalter, the gospels, or her own heart, Nell's example teaches us that we can develop individual forms of breath prayer, each tailored to our own needs and well suited to spiritual practice in city crowds.

When we cannot pray, I'm encouraged by Nell's mention of the seed within: the Holy Spirit, who prays for us, as the New Testament promises. On busy streets or stuck in gridlock traffic, we can be assured that the Holy One is not only hearing our prayers but helping us form them as well.

Spontaneous Prayer

Recently, as I stood on a city street corner waiting for a green light, a bicycle messenger whizzed by, just missing me and two other pedestrians. So close was the cyclist, I could smell the garlic he'd had with lunch.

"Oh, Lord," gasped the woman beside me.

"God, help," I murmured.

There they were: spontaneous prayers offered up on a busy urban corner while a lunch-hour crowd surged and ebbed and surged again. Anthony Bloom, the great spiritual writer and Eastern Orthodox archbishop, speaks of "spontaneous prayer, the kind that gushes out of the our own souls." Sometimes this occurs at moments of danger or desire.[11] Most of us have experienced this at times of fear, need, or longing. This kind of prayer can take us by surprise with its intensity.

In calmer moments, you can summon spontaneous prayer, whether silent, vocal, formal, or informal. Such prayer can be integrated with daily life, if it comes from the heart, which is where you find God, not "out there somewhere," but within: the door at which God constantly knocks.[12]

You can choose a prayer that you can say or repeat inwardly with all your heart, will, mind, and soul; such prayers can be offered silently in the midst of crowded avenues and freeways, shopping malls and stores.[13] There are numerous opportunities for this, times when you pause or wait or walk. Then a prayer word or breath prayer can be interwoven with the fabric of your day.

Nell, the homeless woman who had so little, lived with a constant sense of God's nearness to her, and she resented a social worker who downplayed her spiritual sensibilities. In fact, those sensibilities had been a part of Nell's daily life in her devout childhood home and to her were "nothing special," as she said. She quietly, steadily, maintained a knowing that she was always in God's sight, and to God's presence she was attentive.

I wondered how Nell could maintain this knowing as she moved through every phase of her challenging, uncertain, crowded urban life. If she could have put this attitude into words, she might have said, "That's just how it is."

Secret Prayer

What if Nell's spiritual companion were you?

Holy people aren't necessarily found among the canonized saints, Thomas Kelly reminds us in *A Testament of Devotion,* a spiritual classic. These people quietly maintain "the practice of secret prayer" and are "housewives and hand workers, plumbers and teachers, learned and unlettered, black and white, poor and...rich."[14] And all of them are in the crowds we mingle with in cities.

Can we really be like them? Is it truly possible for us to navigate our way through a crowd and be attentive to God?

"Begin now," writes Kelly. "Walk and talk and laugh with your friends. But behind the scenes, keep up the life of simple prayer and inward worship." Offer what you can, and work on the habit of spiritual attentiveness—allow joy, peace, and wonder to fairly burst from you.[15]

At first, Kelly acknowledges, there's an alternation between attentiveness to the spiritual dimension and inattentiveness. There are many lapses in our mindfulness, our prayerfulness as we begin. Yet "there is a way of ordering our mental life on more than one level at once. On one level we may be thinking, discussing, seeing, calculating, meeting all the demands of external affairs. But deep within, behind the scenes, at a profounder level, we may also be in prayer."[16]

I watch drivers talking on cell phones, making U-turns in city traffic, and marvel at their ability to multitask. It amazes me how people can move through crowds, navigating busy intersections and making the right bus, while their attention seems focused on the BlackBerry in their hands. And then I wonder why I'm surprised that Nell and countless others could maintain a spiritual focus in an urban crowd. Our prayers are secret, in Thomas Kelly's usage, and I like to think of our silent prayers as rising like a cloud above a swarming city street.

Another homeless woman was my teacher. She shared with me an unforgettable image that came to her in dreams as she slept on a mattress, set out with others, on the chapel floor of a Lutheran church. The image came to her until a doctor's medication took away her images and her dreams. Before then, this woman had a persistent vision, a dream of the crowded streets of her city, dim streets, lit by the crowds themselves, with every person wearing a miner's hat with a small lamp on it. The lights, she explained, were from the Spirit of God in each person, and she believed in this light—"the true Light, which lighteth every man" (John 1:9).

This homeless woman had seen miners on television with their lit hats, and she never forgot the sight; it was a mental picture she carried with her thereafter and projected on the cityscape around her. Like Nell, she knew the Bible and remembered the words from John's gospel long after her medication erased her inner visions.

Biblical Crowds

The word *crowd* is derived from the Old English *cruden* or *crod,* both of which signify "a multitude."[17] These words make me think of the multitudes who gathered to hear the Hebrew prophets in cities and who surrounded Moses as he led God's people out of bondage in Egypt. King David danced in a crowd before the ark of the covenant, and of course, the holy temple, built by King Solomon, was located in the great city of Jerusalem, which attracted crowds of pilgrims.

We would be awed, perhaps, if we allowed ourselves to imagine the throngs of people streaming up the temple mount at the time of the Passover. And these holiday crowds are not the only ones in Scripture.

In the book of the prophet Nehemiah, we read: "And all the people gathered themselves together as one man into the street that was before the water gate; and they spake unto Ezra the scribe to bring the book of the law of Moses, which the LORD had commanded to Israel.... And Ezra blessed the LORD, the great God. And all the people answered, Amen, Amen, with lifting up their hands: and they bowed their heads, and worshipped the LORD with their faces to the ground" (8:1, 6). This is the prayer of a crowd; the prayer of many people, close together, lost in God's praise.

Multitudes

In the gospels, there are also multitudes who seek the Holy. Crowds followed Jesus of Nazareth in cities and towns—including Jerusalem, where, He knew, He would die on the cross: a public death, in the presence of more crowds. During His public ministry, Jesus was called by a humble man in a crowd waiting by the side of the Jericho Road. There (see Mark 10:46), the blind beggar Bartimaeus cried out to Jesus. The crowd tried to silence the beggar, but Jesus heard him and, in the midst of the multitudes, turned and healed Bartimaeus.

The gospel of Mark also notes that the multitudes were so plentiful around Jesus that on at least one occasion He had to stand in a boat to address people. All four gospels narrate the miraculous feeding of more than five thousand people who had gathered in a wilderness place to hear Jesus preach, and yet another crowd gathered to hear the Sermon on the Mount.

Sometimes, as I move through metropolitan multitudes, I try to picture these scenes and remind myself that human nature hasn't changed much in two thousand years. We may dress differently, but we're linked to our spiritual ancestors nonetheless. In a way, we're all part of the same great throng of humanity.

A scriptural story with resonance for me, when I am in a city crowd, tells of a woman who had long been ill. "When she had heard of Jesus, [she] came in the press behind, and touched his garment...[and] she was healed of that plague. And Jesus...turned him about in the press, and said, Who touched my clothes? And his disciples said unto him, Thou seest the multitude thronging thee" (Mark 5:27, 29–31). In such a crush of people, that woman still had the courage and faith to reach out for the Holy.

She is my teacher, an example I keep before me.

I also keep before me a contemporary example of soul touching soul: An attractive woman is standing at the curb of an active urban street. The woman, despite her fine features, lovely hair and clothes, looks unhappy. Her troubled gaze is turned inward. She doesn't hear the voice issuing from a taxi: "Hey, beautiful!"

In the taxi is an older woman of nondescript appearance except for the extraordinary radiance of her smile and her face. She repeats her call.

The younger woman, confused, startled, stares vaguely in the direction of the taxi.

For a third time, the passenger calls out, "I said, you look beautiful!"

The younger woman, the pedestrian, hears the words at last and abruptly changes. The troubled, preoccupied look falls away as if a mask has crumbled. A wide smile illuminates her face.

For a moment, the two women just look at each other, like icons that suddenly match, and then the traffic light changes, the taxi lurches away, and the beautiful woman strides across the street as if she has been transformed by a stranger's generosity.

In that moment, I was reminded that the Holy can come to us right where we are, in the midst of multitudes. We don't have to be in a retreat house to sense God's touch. God can reach through you and me not only in privacy but caught in a crush of others, on a street, on a highway, in a cityscape.

This is part of everyone's spiritual legacy, everyone's story, and when I reflect on this truth, I must admit that it comes as something of a shock to me. This is not the venue I expected for a spiritual life, but from history's beginnings it has been that way. This came as no surprise to the pilgrims who flooded the roads to the great pilgrimage cathedrals of the Middle Ages; I learned this early in my education when I studied Chaucer's *Canterbury Tales.* Those pilgrims, and today's pilgrims, didn't expect or perhaps even desire privatized spirituality. Not only was there safety in the community but there was a sense of shared spiritual purpose, which we may have lost in our own time. In crowded elevators and on packed subway trains, on buses and highways and streets, I meet the Holy One I seek in others' faces, if I dare to look.

Time Apart

All over the world, spirituality is practiced among city crowds, in the midst of daily life and work. An example of this comes from the teeming streets of a city in India and an iconic figure of modern prayerfulness. Her words may strike a chord with many of us.

"There are some people who, in order not to pray, use as an excuse the fact that life is so hectic that it prevents them from praying. This cannot be," wrote Mother Teresa of Calcutta. "Prayer does not demand that we interrupt our work, but that we continue working as if it were a prayer."[18] Everything we do, then, can be offered to God in a prayerful way.

If you don't feel comfortable with concepts such as breath prayer, try speaking directly to God. Just speak. Tell Him everything; talk to Him. "He is our father," Mother Teresa said. "He is father to us all whatever religion we are."[19]

And if we still don't know what to say?

"When we have nothing to give [to God], let us give him that nothingness," Mother Teresa suggested in her book *Everything Starts from Prayer.* "God is always speaking to us. Listen to him."[20]

However, even Mother Teresa knew the need for some time apart, for solitude and silence. These periods can be worked into our day, a little time apart from crowds and people; it's notable that the Hebrew prophets periodically withdrew from the crowds to deserts or caves for spiritual refreshment. It's equally clear that Jesus often withdrew from the multitudes to pray alone. After a long period of healing crowds of people, Mark's gospel reports: "And in the morning, rising up a great while before day, he went out, and departed into a solitary place, and there prayed" (Mark 1:35). The disciples found him there and said, "All men seek for thee" (verse 37).

There are times when all people seem to seek for us too, when needs and demands themselves become the crowd—a multitude of calls, messages, orders, obligations, commitments—and all press in upon us. Perhaps it's then that we too must get up a bit earlier, ahead of our busy world, and create some time apart to pray, before the crowd forms around us again and changes the spiritual dynamic.

"We, too, are called to withdraw at certain intervals into deeper… aloneness with God," wrote Mother Teresa. "To be alone with him…to dwell lovingly in his presence."[21] Then we shift modes and practice prayer as did Nell and Kelly and as countless people around us may be doing on every street, bridge, alley, and avenue.

Dark and Light

As He sent His disciples out to the towns of Galilee, Jesus warned His followers to be "wise as serpents, and harmless as doves" (Matthew 10:16). In city crowds, we too must be both. Sometimes in our age spirituality may be mistaken for weakness. We cannot float down an urban street with our wallets or our purses wide open. Practicing the presence of God doesn't mean we lack common sense in a metropolitan throng. Mother Teresa, ministering and praying in Calcutta, is a good example for me of Jesus's mandate. Her spirituality was gritty, not pretty, as she pulled babies from dustbins and as she continued her prayer life.[22]

Crowds, we know well, can have a dark side. Think of those who stoned the prophets in Jerusalem and who nearly pushed Jesus off a cliff in Nazareth. Think of mob rule at various times in urban history in highly civilized countries, including the lynch mobs in our own and in such venerable, beautiful cities as Paris.

We may bear this in mind as we go out into city crowds, which are remarkably orderly, most of the time. And some of the time, they offer us special opportunities for camaraderie. We have enjoyed such scenes televised from the National Mall in Washington DC on the Fourth of July and from cities all over the world on New Year's Eve, where millions of people form congenial crowds.

Awareness of a crowd's potentially dark side does not detract from its many, varied, and rich spiritual opportunities. In fact, such awareness makes it all the more important, I think, that we bring our own spirituality into the street, the freeway, the marketplace. There's something contagious about the peace we can bring to other people by living out of a spiritual grounding ourselves. "Make me an instrument of Your peace," begins the prayer attributed to Saint Francis of Assisi.

And when he cannot feel like the material for such an instrument, J. Brent Bill reminds himself that "the fellow that grabbed the first loaf of bread with its freshly baked aroma is standing in front of me, smiling at his young son. The young woman who cut me off on the freeway could be my daughter as surely as she is someone else's."[23]

Transcendent Moments

Occasionally, something happens in an urban crowd that transcends the ordinary. Sometimes there's a moment of grace that seems like divine intervention and, in a flash, lifts everyone's spirituality.

In 2007, on a packed subway platform in New York City, an epileptic man fell onto the tracks. In the few seconds before an oncoming train roared into the station, a man came from the crowd and threw his body over the epileptic man. The train rushed over them both, while the hero of this hour held the trembling man still in the small space just beneath the bottom of the subway cars. This action saved a life, made the evening news, and inspired a city.

Wesley Autrey, the man who intervened, later said that anyone would do what he had done.

Perhaps.

But it's in urban crowds that we are offered such opportunities. Autrey's heroism is prayer turned visible and active.

In the metropolis, with its crowds, we're so frequently challenged to hear again the famous words of Matthew 25:35–36, 40: "For I was a hungred, and ye gave me meat: I was thirsty, and ye gave me drink: I was a stranger, and ye took me in: naked, and ye clothed me: I was sick, and ye visited me: I was in prison, and ye came unto me…. And the King shall…say unto them…, Inasmuch as ye have done it unto one of the least of these my brethren, ye have done it unto me."

I will bless the LORD at all times: his praise shall continually be
in my mouth.
My soul shall make her boast in the LORD: the humble shall hear
thereof, and be glad.
O magnify the LORD with me, and let us exalt his name together.
I sought the LORD, and he heard me, and delivered me from all
my fears. (Psalm 34:1–4)

CURES FOR *Soulsickness* IN THE CITY

Stop: Read and Receive

1. How do I feel or not feel energized or overwhelmed by crowded urban streets or shopping districts?

2. In what way do I look at other people in crowds? How can I keep from insulating myself and removing myself from others by staying within my own space?

3. How do I balance necessary vigilance over my personal possessions, such as my wallet or purse, with a compassionate stance toward others?

4. When have I experienced anything like Thomas Merton's "Vision of Louisville"? How did I feel lovingly connected to other people in an urban crowd? How can I be more mindful of my fellowship with others to experience this again or anew?

Yield: Reflect, Journal, or Discuss

5. Begin to see God in each person you pass in a crowd. Practice this slowly for one block, then two blocks, then more.

6. Pray silently in a crowd. Deliberately note when you're too intent on holding your own in an urban setting.

7. Look over a packed concert hall or a line at a movie theater and pray a blessing on the people gathered with you.

8. Ask yourself: Is it easier for me to pray for the vulnerable people in a crowd (the elderly, the homeless, children) than it is for me to pray for those who look well off and well dressed?

Go: Experience and Engage

9. In city crowds, imagine how you're connected invisibly to those around you.

10. When you're walking downtown or in urban settings, try this mental exercise: imagine being part of a crowd swarming around Jesus. Do you behave differently? Is your attitude different? Note these times in a journal.

11. Formulate your own breath prayer, that simple prayer or heart cry that can be said in a single breath while walking, riding in an elevator, or waiting for a light to change or the train to come. Write a list of breath prayers.

12. When you feel small and anonymous in a city crowd, remember, and repeat silently, God's words to Isaiah: "I have called thee by thy name; thou art mine" (43:1). Write this on a file card and put it in your pocket so you can recall the scripture through the day.

3

FINDING GOD IN NOISE
The Gateway to Stillness

The city always speaks. Always. When I've lived in large urban centers, my first instinct was to fight the noise, shut it out, fend it off, keep it away. I remember cringing once as screeching brakes pierced the prayerful silence in a downtown house of worship. Another time I neared tears as I tried to pray in an apartment. My soothing spiritual music was obliterated by the din of jackhammers and the honking of horns outside. And there are certain urban ironies: the coincidental scream of sirens just as the new fire of an Easter vigil is kindled in a downtown church courtyard; the crack during a sermon of a fender bender outside another church.

Even when I looked for apartments on buildings' higher floors, I couldn't escape a city's natural roar. On the streets it's impossible to avoid the screech of brakes, shouts of vendors, and the constant sound of many voices: "No right turn!" "Hey, girl!" "Pretzels!" "News!" "Discounts!" "Waxing!" "Chestnuts!" "Samples!"

Help!

My first response: White-noise machines. Earplugs. Companies who specialize in double-paned windows to diminish the city's sound volume (which apparently bothers others as well). The highest floor I could afford (not high enough). No cell phone (I had to give way on this one).

I'd been told repeatedly that I'd get used to the sounds of the city. After a while, I was assured, I wouldn't even hear the jackhammers and sirens that make short work of white-noise machines and can sometimes penetrate those expensive windowpanes. How, I wondered, could a person have a prayer life with so much sensory overload? Is such a notion even possible?

It *is* possible, of course, and I've learned this, despite my initial resistance.

The truth is, when we begin the discipline of trying to see God in others, it follows naturally that we begin to hear God's voice in others as well. We are imperfect instruments, to be sure, but if we listen to the city from a spiritual stance, we might be surprised at what we discern. Behind each urban sound is a story, a life, a human soul.

One day I stood watching some construction workers laboring to repair a busy urban street. United Parcel Service trucks began to pile up around the workers.

"Bad guys," a kid shouted from the sidewalk and, I'm sure, there were adult passersby who felt equal annoyance.

A worker looked up into a scowling face and, shaking his head, looked away. He was, perhaps, doing what seemed like a thankless job. And yet I was struck by how much energy and labor he generated before my eyes.

And ears. We can, in fact, cultivate a prayerful sense of gratitude for the operators of backhoes and jackhammers who are toiling on our behalf and for our cities' safety. After watching those people behind the Men at Work signs, I see them in my mind's eye now whenever I hear the sounds of their labor. This is an attitude that takes daily practice—for me, at any rate—but paradoxically, the noise doesn't seem as loud when I don't tense against it, when I try to sense God's presence in the midst of the din—the "still small voice" after the whirlwind (see 1 Kings 19:11–13).

The scream of a siren has never been the same to me since the afternoon I saw a man lying on the asphalt of a much-traveled street. He had just been hit by a car, and an ambulance was opening its doors to him. Soon it would be wailing its way to an emergency room with the unconscious man on its gurney. I still see the man's ashen face. From that time forward, I've tried to say a silent prayer, a "siren prayer," whenever I hear a siren—a practice urged upon me long ago but that I'd allowed to lapse for a time. Now each siren has become a distress call raised up to the "congregation" of us in the city through siren prayer, and I feel more connected to God and others.

This kind of praying is something anyone can learn to do, and it does allow the urban noise to lead us into a greater sensitivity to others. In most cities, if we use sirens as cues, we find ourselves in prayer more often; the sound becomes a gateway to prayer, rather than an obstacle.

When horns honk, we can also avoid tensing against the sound, sharp as it may be. We've all been impatient—there must be universal empathy with that. I recall running down a street through a summer rain, calling for a taxi. I didn't look behind me but later learned I'd cut off a few other pedestrians who wanted a taxi as well.

I remember my face grew hot as I thought about this—how impatient I was, how thoughtless. How much I had in common with the frustrated drivers. Now, when I hear the honking of horns below my apartment, I try to remember that each sound represents a human life, a life that could be mine, or my friend's, or my sister's or brother's. And, in the larger scheme of things, of course, they are. Each life is part of the city's mosaic, and every life has its own voice, its own song, its own importance to God.

Cities Within Cities

Once I spent time as a summer chaplain intern in a big urban hospital. This place itself was like a city within a city, with its own rush and bustle, and almost continuous noise. Loudspeakers paged staff members, trays of food and medicines rattled, beepers and bells sounded, phones rang, voices spoke and murmured and called. People moaned and cried in pain. Medical machines hummed, buzzed, and purred.

As a layperson assisting a chaplain, I often wondered how anyone could get well in such an environment. As a miniature city, neither it nor its larger model seemed a healing locale. And in the hospitals, it seemed as if the time was always rush hour.

I most enjoyed my night shifts, when the hospital was quieter and I could move quietly, almost invisibly about my work in assistance, like the Spirit on the stairwell. But I also learned how to handle the noise of the hospital's daily routine, just as I have had to learn how to handle the sounds of a city.

"This is life," a nurse told me as she pushed a jangling medications cart. "On the outside, on the inside, that's how it is."

There was also comfort for me in thinking of my father, a busy surgeon. He went about his hospital rounds and bedside visits with a serenity born of his love for medicine and his devotion to his patients. In fact, my earliest memory is of sound: the phone ringing in the middle of the night, so many nights, and the rustlings and clinks and footsteps as my father rose, dressed, and went out into the darkness on a house call, long past the time when house calls were routinely made in Manhattan and the Bronx.

I also recall my father's deep exhaustion at the end of many days, most days. A man of science, a fierce atheist, he had no spiritual well on which to draw—and emphatically, intentionally, he didn't want one. I've often thought that somewhere, deep within, he needed this; much later, as I entered his territory in a different city, I knew for certain that this need, present since I can remember, would always be with me. How to fill it amid a noisy city or an urban hospital?

I consulted the chaplain of one metro hospital, an experienced Methodist minister who had been following his vocation for more than thirty years. He looked me up and down with a professional, diagnostic gaze as I waited anxiously for the wisdom I knew he would impart.

"Take breaks," he said finally. "They might be short, they might not be the Transfiguration on the mountain, but make them silent." He peered over his glasses then and repeated, "Breaks. Take them."

Taking Breaks

Encouraged by this mentor, I learned to spend part of each lunch hour in the chapel in silence. Then I spent more time sitting quietly with the patients I visited; when asked for prayer, I also began to learn the pleasure of praying in silence with another person.

I tried another practice too. Because I was required to wash my hands after being with every patient, I began to use that time for quick, silent prayer—prayer for the person I'd just visited and the person I'd see next, and prayer that I might be present to that next patient and to God. These small breaks for quiet prayer made an increasing difference to me.

What about you? How often have you found yourself in noisy situations? How have you found quiet in them—or not?

However you've handled those kinds of scenarios in the past may help you seek quiet, within and without, in the urban landscape.

Being and Doing

My city hospital experiences remind me again that there is a difference between "being" and "doing." Another chaplain intern was unaccustomed to quiet time. In fact, he was uncomfortable with the idea of simply "being," or "being with" someone else. He wanted to fix what was broken, and if he couldn't fix the situation, he admitted, he didn't want to be in it. Problem solving was his approach. But our supervisor's patient counsel slowly effected a change in this chaplain intern, the kind of change Thomas Merton describes in *Conjectures of a Guilty Bystander.*

"We are so obsessed with *doing* that we have no time and no imagination left for *being*," Merton wrote. "As a result, men are valued not for what they are but for what they *do* or what they *have*—for their usefulness.… Those who relinquish God as the center of their moral orbit lose all direction."[1]

I can see how that can be a great temptation, especially with a city's many loud distractions around us. How easy it is to lose a sense of centeredness on God, to spin off in too many directions, to look busy. Creating sound can be a sign of *doing* something, of being in demand, important, needed, even powerful. We may even secretly suspect that *being* is for "losers," for the weak, for the insignificant. It's important to examine our resistance to silence, to quiet prayerfulness. Do we suppose that silent prayerfulness is only for cloistered contemplatives? It may surprise us to recall that some of the world's most active people were quietly prayerful, from Abraham Lincoln to Martin Luther King Jr., from Florence Nightingale to Harriet Tubman. And there are many such people that we will never know about.

In the end, what matters is how we feel about God when we make silent spiritual time, as a part of life. After reading the accounts of those who live this way, it's easy to receive an impression of the lasting joy, peace, and meaning available to us all. For us, these benefits are rooted in prayer and, when we can't find it around us, inner silence.

Inner Noise

When you think about it, you realize everyone has chatter going on in their heads. Today, for anyone with a cell phone, silence is especially elusive.

"We live in an age of sound," writes Claudia Horwitz in *The Spiritual Activist*. "At work, telephones ring, machines hum, people talk, faxes fax. We come home and we turn on our radios, televisions, CD players, and VCRs. We can barely imagine our life without this wall of noise."[2]

To deal with walls of noise, I received a suggestion from another mentor: use imagery, at first, to still the mind. In silence, he said, we often find ourselves thinking of things we forgot to do, should be doing—must do. Before we know it, an entire to-do list takes shape in our consciousness. In silence, we can generate our own noise: enough to compete with honking horns and screaming sirens.

For me this happens more frequently in cities, where noise is the order of the day. But this mentor knew how to achieve inner quiet even as he ministered in the noisy world of an urban jail; it was he who helped me with that prelude to prayer: stilling the mind.

At the start of each day, he told me and other volunteers to sit in silence together and become aware of our breathing. Then he suggested that we imagine a coatrack on a wall, where we could put all our to-do lists, all our concerns and mental clutter, as well as our doubts and anxieties.

We were to visualize our coats and hang them up on that imaginary rack. "Put it over there, with all its pockets, linings, and stuff," he said. "No one wants your coat. It'll be there when the day's over. Meanwhile, hang it up, put it over there. That's what you do with some of your own stuff, if it gets in the way." He also recommended that we refrain from asking God to fix the coat while it hung there on that rack because this exercise was not about petition but about clearing our minds to focus on God.

This practice has helped me and others.

For you, it might be helpful to imagine all your mental baggage as packages or bundles placed on a safe shelf or as a ball of string put into the hands of a friend who will hold it for you while you go into your quiet time. The simpler the image, the better. This is simply a way to enter that inner sanctuary remarked upon with gratitude by many ordinary pray-ers and everyday seekers.

The Sound of Silence

Silence can be uncomfortable for some people. I've known city dwellers who aren't at ease with the deep nighttime hush of the country and its all-encompassing darkness. The late Fred Ebb of the musical team Kander and Ebb (*Cabaret; Chicago; New York, New York*) was thoroughly urban, and the story goes that he kept his back to the window when he made his one visit to Kander's country home. The countryside probably was too quiet for Ebb, and it was certainly not the city habitat he loved.

All the same, if we're to sustain and maintain a spiritual life, we do need to make time for external and internal silence, and we can do this in our own homes and offices. Thomas Kelly writes of a busy executive who scheduled calendar time for silence, prayer, and meditation. Mother Teresa wrote about cultivating "the silence of the heart":

> Silence of the heart, not only of the mouth—that too is necessary.
>   Then you can hear God everywhere:
> in the closing of the door, in the person who needs you,
> in the birds that sing,
> in the flowers, the animals—
> that silence which is wonder and praise.[3]

You've probably heard of people who say that sitting in silence for twenty minutes drives them crazy. Why is silence threatening to some of us? Perhaps it carries with it the connotation of loneliness, or rejection, or abandonment.

I had a neighbor once in an upstairs apartment who kept her television on all night long—for company, I think. Then again, perhaps silence caused her (like many of us) to face herself: her mistakes and losses, her hurts and anger—and this was too painful. Sometimes, without distractions, such emotions do surface; when they do, our first instinct may be to escape, to distract ourselves.

Resting the Mind

Cities offer so many distractions for the senses, and many of those come as sound, not only the sounds of the metropolis, but of gadgets and technologies like ringing cell phones, clicking iPods, the beeps and blings of instant messaging, and alarms on wristwatches.

But if you sincerely want to learn to pray, Mother Teresa wrote, keep silent: "Interior silence is very difficult but you must make the effort. In silence we will find new energy and true unity. The energy of God will be ours to do all things well."[4]

Spiritual people of all traditions have known the relationship between quiet and prayer, and it need not be feared. In fact, as you grow used to it, you can find yourself wanting more of its refreshment, the space it makes for encounters with God. You can discover peace, the peace that the world doesn't give, the peace that Jesus promises. More important still is the experience of God's loving presence, once you find that still point where you can sense the presence of the Holy One.

I find the technique of "centering prayer" very helpful, practiced for twenty minutes, twice a day. Centering prayer allows you to focus on a word for the Holy, or perhaps a symbol holy to you, like a cross or a candle flame. This does require discipline and often a closed door, but the practice of contemplation opens the heart to the presence of God. Interestingly, as you make time for silence, you'll become aware of your own mental clamor. This is when it's important to be patient with yourself and simply, gently, return your attention to your focal point—God. You might become more aware of noise around you at first, but the practice becomes easier and more nourishing to the spirit the more you exercise it.

"As I silence myself, I become more sensitive to the sounds around me and I do not block them out," Tayeko Yamanouchi writes. "The songs of the birds, the rustle of the wind, children in the playground, the roar of an airplane overhead are all taken into my worship.... I think of myself like the tree planted by the 'rivers of water' in Psalm One, sucking up God's gift of life and being restored."[5]

Contemplative prayer is, of course, far more than a skill to be mastered. It's not simply mechanical concentration or a mental fitness routine. It comes from the heart and the emotions, according to great spiritual writers. Speech too can be prayerful, if these are its source. "Though I speak with the tongues of men and of angels, and have not charity, I am become as sounding brass, or a tinkling cymbal," writes Paul (1 Corinthians 13:1).

Quiet Time with God

Sometimes, when waiting for a bus to come or a light to change or the phone to ring, you can feel it, even through the staccato beat of a city. It's that longing that you can deny for only so long, the longing to be in the presence of something greater than yourself, that presence you suspect is waiting for you all the time.

"We spend our days and nights in a vague loneliness for someone or something to make us feel complete," notes Emilie Griffin. "Many people divert this longing into kinds of self-gratification, hoping to still the restlessness."[6]

This feeling is "Godsickness," writes Evelyn Underhill—something like homesickness.[7] As quoted in chapter 1, Augustine of Hippo, who had "everything" the world could give, famously reflected, "O God, you have made us for yourself, and our hearts are restless until they find their rest in you."[8]

As Griffin points out, we need some kind of structure if we're to seek God's presence in silence. In her book *Doors into Prayer*, she tells of a university chaplain who schedules two mornings a week for prayer, like Thomas Kelly's busy executive. There are people on Wall Street who feel burned out and seek such times, such respites.[9] For example, Griffin says, the parent of young children may find the best time for such prayerful quiet is right after the school bus leaves. Griffin is a mother herself and, when finding her way spiritually in New York City, would go into churches at lunchtime to pray for a quarter hour or so. Later, in a fast-paced office in New Orleans, she would go to a public formal garden where she experienced silence and peace.[10]

Where you go to be quietly prayerful is a highly individual choice. The first step, of course, is making the decision to set aside the time. Once you select the time and place, make a covenant with yourself that you'll show up there. After a while, you'll come to look forward to these periods when you can feel God's presence and love, as well as your own love for God.

Sense of Presence

I heard an intriguing story of a woman's experience of prayerfulness. She came to her minister to complain: she had been practicing vocal prayer for fourteen years and still didn't feel God's presence. Her minister advised her to arrange her room peacefully, close the door, and take up her familiar knitting in the silence. Soon the woman returned with delight.

"It works," she reported. When asked to describe what was working, the woman said that she would focus on her knitting and become quiet inside with only the noise around her being the click of her needles. "This silence was not simply an absence of noise, but had substance," she noticed. "It was not the absence of something, but the presence of something—the silence had a density, a richness, and it began to pervade.... At the heart of the silence, there was He who is all stillness, peace, all poise."[11]

Instead of being so intent on *doing,* this woman learned to *be.* She learned to be in God's presence.

This is like the story told by a Catholic priest of France, the Curé d'Ars, about a peasant who used to spend hours and hours sitting in the chapel motionless, doing nothing.

The priest said to the peasant, "What are you doing all these hours?"

The old peasant said, "I look at Him, He looks at me, and we are happy.'"[12]

Perhaps we think that this isn't possible for us, but we can rest assured that many people, in many cities, and in many historical periods, have gone before us into the silence for time with God and emerged centered, anchored, and softened.

"He gives an amazing stayedness in Him," writes Thomas Kelly, "a well-nigh unbroken life of humble quiet adoration in His presence, at the depths of our being. And night, winter and summer, He is here, the great Champion. And we are with Him, held in His tenderness, quickened into quietness and peace."[13]

Why Spiritual Silence?

His tenderness can bring about physical benefits. In *Finding God in Unexpected Places,* Philip Yancey notes Dr. David Larson's study on health and Christian commitment. Larson found that regular church attendees have a lower incidence of heart attack, arteriosclerosis, and high blood pressure.[14]

But this certain good news is not the reason that the woman "knitted before God" or the French peasant sat gazing. It's not the reason for Saint Augustine's restless heart or Evelyn Underhill's Godsickness either.

The reason, Methodist pastor A. W. Tozer explains, is this: "As we begin to focus on God, the things of the spirit will take shape before our inner eyes. It will give acute perception enabling us to see God even as is promised to the pure in heart. A new God-consciousness will seize upon us and we shall begin to taste and hear and inwardly feel God, who is our life and our all. There will be the constant shining of 'the true Light, which lighteth every man that cometh into the world' (John 1:9)."[15]

This kind of focus often comes in silence: silence that we can make in the midst of our city lives. Wherever we are, we can speak to God in the words of Thomas Merton: "To be here with the silence of Sonship in my heart is to be a center in which all things converge upon you.... Therefore, Father, I beg you to keep me in this silence so that I may learn from it, the word of your peace and the word of your mercy and the word of your gentleness to the world: and that through me perhaps your word of peace may make itself heard where it has not been possible for anyone to hear it for a long time."[16]

Each of us can be a "word of peace" on the street, in the subway, on the freeway, on the crosstown bus.

When I let myself, I can often find this kind of peace, this kind of stillness, even in the busy city. I find it on what seem to be islands of silence around each individual in a cluster of people on a street corner. We wait together—for a light, for a store to open, for a bus or a subway train—and in that collection of silence, or those "islands," there is a shared peace. We share the space, the situation, and for those moments are silent together, which paradoxically is not on islands after all. I've had this feeling at noisy intersections and in crowded elevators, where people stand patiently, quietly, unified by the situation and shared presence.

Once, when I was a child, I experienced this. Part of a jostling, joyous throng on Manhattan's Central Park West, I waited with my father to view Macy's Thanksgiving Day Parade. I was about five and could see nothing until he lifted me onto his shoulders. Suddenly I was looking into the eyes of other kids, similarly hoisted high. No one said a word. Beneath me I could feel my father's strength. All noise seemed to fade away. There was only my father and my wonderstruck peers and the huge sky that seemed to be within our reach.

I think of that moment often in prayer, especially in trying times. I think of God holding me up and lifting me into a peaceful place.

"Friendly silence speaks—yes, *speaks,* oddly enough, to the hunger for silence that we see in people all around us," writes J. Brent Bill in *Holy Silence.* "There's rising interest in silent retreats and contemplative reading. Something in our souls tells us that getting quiet is a good way to meet God."[17]

That silence restores the soul, Bill says.[18]

It also restores relationships. Think of times when you want to be close to a friend or your spouse. You seldom meet in a noisy place, but rather in a quiet venue where you can hear each other. And as that relationship grows, the more you crave to spend quiet time with the beloved.

Should it be so different with God, with whom we have a relationship?

This is possible for each of us who wants it and listens; it's present in groups of waiting people on every city street, and it's within each one of us, as we grow in our attentiveness to God's presence, wherever we are.

Scripture and Silence

Imagine ancient Jerusalem, celebrated as the mother of all cities and called, by the prophet Ezekiel, the center of the earth. This city is the image used by scriptural writers for heaven and the one the builders of the great churches at Chartres wanted to evoke as the heavenly Jerusalem.

Yet ancient Jerusalem was hardly a city of silence. People entered by many gates and the streets crisscrossed; busy markets attracted the traffic of people, camels, and donkeys, and yet… the center of Jerusalem held a sacred silence in the great temple's most holy place. The surrounding sounds of the great city must have set off the holy silence all the more.

The prophet Elijah understood that holy silence. It was Elijah who recognized God's presence, not in thunder, earthquake, or fire, but in stillness. The point is, God's voice doesn't necessarily come dramatically when we're removed, but rather He is there always, in our midst (see 1 Kings 19:11–13). He's there for us today, in our cities' stop-and-go rhythms; He's there in the quiet clusters of those who pause, gaze, and wait; He's in the hush before a curtain goes up in a theater, and in the centers of our own spirits.

In the book of Acts, an amazing occurrence is recorded after the resurrection of Jesus. At the Feast of Pentecost, Christ's disciples experienced an unexpected miracle: the harmony of many urban voices, each speaking in its own language, "out of every nation under heaven"—and everyone understood one another. The Holy Spirit descended upon Jerusalem's multitudes and still provides an inspiration to those who seek spirituality through the medium of sound (see Acts 2:1–12).

It's easy to forget that the context for Jesus's ministry and that of the disciples was so often a town or city. We forget too that the Hebrew prophets were not always in mountainous caves but moved about in cities and towns; throughout history, they, like the people they addressed, have been able to find silence within.

Finding City Silence

Although we don't have caves enclosed within our cities, we do have parks of all sizes and shapes—good places, perhaps, to find a slice of silence to sweeten the day—and we have a corner of our home, or perhaps a home office.

In the film *Place*, author Thomas Moore interviews people who find quiet sacred space in even smaller, more contained spaces within where they live: in a workroom, at a hearthside, in a favorite chair.[19]

"God was waiting in the depths of my being to talk to me if I would only get still enough to hear His voice," successful businessman Martin Hope Sutton writes in describing his place for connecting with God. "I had no sooner commenced than a perfect pandemonium of voices reached my ears, a thousand clamoring notes from without and within, until I could hear nothing but their noise and din."[20]

Does this sound familiar to you? Is this your experience of the silent times you've sought with God? Do you feel the city drowning out your concentration, your connection?

For Sutton, attempts to connect eventually grew easier. He listened again and again to God's promise. "God said, 'Be still and know that I am God.'" And as Sutton persevered, he says, "There was a still, small voice in the depths of my being that began to speak with an inexpressible tenderness, power, and comfort.... It became to me the voice of prayer, and the voice of wisdom and I did not need to think so hard, or pray so hard, or trust so hard, but that 'still small voice' of the Holy Spirit in my heart was God's prayer in my secret soul, was God's answer to all my questions."[21]

In cityscapes, sacred silence is everywhere, once you begin to listen for it: before the household is awake, in the shower, on the bus, in the line at the bank—and in the area you create specially as your own chapel of the heart, for a deeper, longer time focused on the One who always waits for you to ask, to knock, to be present.

Time and Tides

All cities have tides of noise and relative quiet. I savor those moments when the muted sounds of the metropolis itself become a kind of prayer. In summer, most cities empty out and become more still as people leave to go on vacations at the shore or the mountains or abroad. I like those summer evenings when the stars seem to touch the skyscrapers, and the skyscrapers seem like reaching fingers, and the city's voice reminds me of the words, "As it was in the beginning, is now, and ever shall be, world without end."

In most urban areas, there are certain hours in early morning when the city's lights glimmer silently like strands of gems. So Paris is often described. The buildings are silhouetted against the sky, and one thinks of the millions of people they shelter, holding us, somehow, under one roof, however jagged. City streets have often been compared to canyons, and at five in the morning, the buildings might be mountains or cliffs or sentinels.

I remember, as an older child and later in high school, when my father took me on house calls with him. He would step into what seemed a softer, quieter dark, and out of this darkness always came the voice of the policeman on the beat: "Morning to ya, Doctor."

My father often had patients to visit in Harlem, and I remember the shine of a street light on the cross of a storefront church, the grates pulled down over the silent shops, the shattered glass that made the pavement sparkle. There seemed to be so many crosses, so many small, humble churches. We would slow down to look at them because they always caught my attention and held my gaze.

I remember my silent thankfulness to God for these moments with my father and the city he so loved. And I remember a special sense of God's love as well, as I sensed my father's unspoken affection. That's holy time that I carry with me into my busier, noisier urban day. In the midst of it all, I revisit that holy hush in silence, in gratitude, in prayer.

―――⚬⚬⚬―――

Make a joyful noise unto God, all ye lands:
Sing forth the honour of his name: make his praise glorious....
All the earth shall worship thee, and shall sing unto thee; they
*   shall sing to thy name. (Psalm 66:1–2, 4)*

O clap your hands, all ye people; shout unto God with the voice
*   of triumph....*
For God is the King of all the earth: sing ye praises with under-
*   standing. (Psalm 47:1, 7)*

CURES FOR *Soulsickness* IN THE CITY

Stop: Read and Receive

1. Do I feel distracted and overwhelmed by city sounds, or do they seem like an exciting hum, maybe even an urban hymn, of life itself?

2. How can I begin to think of city sounds as a sign of other human beings and their precious lives all around me? What story does each sound have to tell?

3. What first goes through my mind when I hear certain urban noises, such as the wail of an ambulance or fire truck siren? How can I begin to use these calls as cues to say a brief prayer for people in danger and those who help them?

4. If I hear a jackhammer or a police bullhorn or other intrusive sounds of city workers, in what ways can I begin to practice compassion for the person toiling for my city? Name at least two.

Yield: Reflect, Journal, or Discuss

5. When I hear vendors' cries mingle with beggars' calls, do I tend to shut out the sounds, or do I hear the echo of my voice raised in need?

6. How can I use metropolitan noise as a way to remember the disciples' experience of the first Pentecost after the Resurrection? How can I ever marvel at the way the Holy Spirit weaves together so many ethnic expressions in a city?

7. What kind of voice do I raise in the gigantic chorus of my city? In what three ways might I make my voice kinder, gentler, more patient?

8. How and when are my mind and spirit cluttered with inner self-talk? Am I able to maintain a prayerful, inner silence for brief periods of time—and let them grow longer?

Go: Experience and Engage

9. Converse silently with God while moving about your city today or commuting to and from there. Journal, as to a friend, about opening your heart to God along the way.

10. Make a chart on a piece of paper by drawing a line down the middle. On the left side, list at least three specific situations that try your patience in the midst of metropolitan traffic. Now on the right side, corresponding to each situation, list three short prayers that can help you in each of those times. Tuck this chart in your pocket or purse for easy access in each situation. Today, pray in the noise of the city.

11. If people in elevators or restaurants or on public transportation talk loudly and even rudely, how do you respond? Write out three ways you intend this week to respond in patience.

12. For five minutes, practice making yourself an island of peace in a noisy city. Then practice this for ten minutes. See how long and how often you can do this while moving about downtown.

FINDING GOD IN HASTE

The Gateway to Deliberation

I s there time for God anymore in the urban pace of living?" I asked
a city-bred friend recently. Does this much haste on a continuous
basis leave any time for reflection, recollection, or spirituality, even
when you long for it?

My friend, now an ex-urbanite, simply laughed.

So I prepared to ask a busy city minister this question; first I inquired
about how he was doing amid his many appointments on a tightly scheduled morning. "How am I?" He looked startled by the question. "I have
no idea, no time to check."

Too many of us have this experience as we run our race with the city
clock.

Racing the clock seems to be an especially fast and furious game in
a city. In most locales, of course, there are many kinds of deadlines and
time lines and long lines. Modern life, obviously, is increasingly rushed
and hurried. The pace, however, has always ticked more quickly, more

consistently fast, in urban settings. And now, with the technological revolution, that pace seems more like a race than ever.

We dodge and dart and speed on freeways. In some cities, it's said, we take our lives in our hands whenever we get behind the wheel. We rush across streets before the light has turned green, or we get nudged off the curb by a surge of hastening pedestrians. We hover impatiently in restaurants, awaiting an empty table, or a place on an escalator. "Hold the elevator," we shout, on the run, before the full car's doors can close. We plunge down shortcuts by taxi or foot, and if a subway train is late, we check our watches and tread back and forth on the platform.

Just as there's such a phenomenon as crowd-sickness, there's a syndrome called "hurry-sickness": a compulsion to do everything with greater speed, in the shortest time period.

In his best-selling book *Faster,* James Gleick says that we live in a "world of instantaneity: instant coffee, instant intimacy, instant replay, and instant gratification. We are in a rush. We are making haste. *Gridlocked* and *tarmacked* are metonyms of our era."[1]

In the film *You've Got Mail,* actress Parker Posey's character, Patricia, epitomizes the *Faster* syndrome. She is the very incarnation of a driven, hurried, harried urban person. "Oooh, I'm late," she begins, a bit like the Mad Hatter, and then rattles off a litany of observations so quickly it's difficult to keep up with her. "Hurry, hurry, hurry," she commands the espresso maker.

Her boyfriend later comments, "Patricia makes *coffee* nervous."[2]

Hollywood is not slow to present us with images of our frenetic urban selves.

For me, metropolitan haste is as much a challenge to personal spirituality as crowds and noise. When rushed and rattled, I find it harder to connect both spiritually and physically. We're all different though. There are folks enlivened by a quick pace. In fact, they would tell you the liveliness is magnetic; this is the pace that helps to make a city a happening place, vital and alive.

"Wow," one pedestrian told another on a quiet Sunday downtown. "It's, like, totally *dead* here today."

My father used to find cities "eerie," if not "dead," in the summer when people went on holiday and life slowed down.

There's no doubt about the struggle for a pace somewhere between eerie and frenetic; many people struggle to strike a balance between the city's speed and the soul's need to pause, to pray, to replace.

God Makes Time

In "Stopping by Woods on a Snowy Evening," poet Robert Frost comments on an unusual pause in a journey. This beloved poem, despite its rural setting, speaks to the tension city dwellers feel most acutely between haste and spiritual respite. How beautiful it is to pause contemplatively, Frost observes, and how brief, how temporary such pauses may be:

> The woods are lovely, dark and deep
> But I have promises to keep,
> And miles to go before I sleep,
> And miles to go before I sleep.[3]

When we come upon those woods, in whatever form they take for us, the cause is God's gift and grace. Frost's rural experience can be recaptured even in the city: a spiritual pause while waiting for an elevator, a green light, a subway train. I've learned to cultivate those waiting times and hold fast to them as moments of reverence, like the time I came around a corner onto a tree-lined city street and was struck by the way the light filtered through the leaves. Such a pause seizes me, quite often in a time of crisis.

This was the case for a movie producer portrayed in the film *Grand Canyon*. The producer experiences a moment of grace in Los Angeles, where gazing from his hospital window he sees a sunrise illuminate the city. Deeply moved, he swears off producing any more violent scripts, and his resolution does last...until he recovers. Then the transcendent moment is trivialized, and life is back to business as usual for him.[4]

Can we wait for graced moments to bless or seize us, as surely they will? And can we find ways to open ourselves, intentionally, to God's presence amid our hectic daily lives, even though we too have many "promises to keep and miles to go before [we] sleep, and miles to go before [we] sleep"?

Postponing God

Sometimes, we delay this intention until that very last mile before we sleep. "I think some people put off spirituality until retirement, or even later," observed a busy film producer and longtime friend. "They may think it's something they'll get around to when there's nothing else to do."

Volunteer work in a city hospice made me reflect on this thoughtful opinion. In the hospice atmosphere, which is surprisingly positive and bright, I had to come to terms with the importance of a consistent spiritual life before that final mile.

"You'll wonder why you didn't make more time for that," a patient commented on her prayer life after her minister's visit. "But when you get to where I'm at," she went on, "you can't change what's behind you." The room was filled with flowers and splashed with long, low sunlight that was already fading. And then the woman said something I will always remember: "All that God-time you miss, and you think it doesn't matter. Then."

Another woman in that hospice confided that she felt sorry for herself. A beautiful woman; still, she knew she was dying. There she lay, with her elegant cheekbones and her Foley catheter and her regrets that she was not better prepared for this final season.

"Maybe if I'd prayed more often, I'd know how now," she murmured.

When I came on my shift two weeks later, as I expected, both women were gone.

It's been three years since they shared their feelings with me, but I remember their voices very clearly. I even recall the question of the second woman, who asked me for the name of the perfume I was wearing. I hesitated, not wanting to tell her. She asked a second time. "Eternity,"

I said finally. And we stared at each other. I was actually wearing an invisible essence called Eternity, and the irony was not lost of either of us.

This would not have surprised William Wordsworth who knew, long before Calvin Klein titled his perfume:

> Our birth is but a sleep and a forgetting. The Soul that rises with us, our life's Star, hath had elsewhere its setting and cometh from afar: not in entire forgetfulness, and not in utter nakedness, but trailing clouds of glory do we come from God, who is our home.[5]

That moment in the hospice has stayed with me. I'd not expected it to surface again when I sat with a friend who, like me, is a member of the baby-boomer generation. We spoke of our work at one of the city's universities, and we spoke of the Italian food before us—and we spoke, as well, about this season in our lives.

"For the first time," she observed, without a trace of self-pity, "the finish line just isn't so distant, so 'out there.' So out of sight." Come to think of it, I was wearing Eternity that day as well. I just didn't think about this in that sun-drenched café, with the clink of forks and the smell of garlic and the sense of endless days ahead for me and my friend. I didn't think about Eternity until she mentioned the finish line and we paused, thinking together about the years that lay before us. *Would I use those years to make more time with God?*

I realized, during this lunch, that the answer mattered in a way it never had before.

And yet, making regular time for God is not a life insurance policy of the sacred kind. As we well know, we don't get "points" for prayer. We don't get a spiritual bank balance to draw on when we reach that last mile. What we get, quite simply, is what the hospice patient said. "More God-time." More of God. More time with the One who loves us beyond all other loves, the mystics tell us, and whose company can be our delight; this is also an age-old witness.

Busy Living

"Life is busy," writes Frederick Buechner in *The Hungering Dark*. "It comes at you like a great wave and if you handle things right, you manage to keep your head above water and go tearing along with it, but if you are not careful, you get pulled under and rolled to the point where you no longer know who you are or where you are going." In many ways that's fine and proper, he adds, "but there are other things about life that are also fine and proper."[6]

He was wise enough to recognize a special moment of God's presence on a late winter afternoon on his way to teach a class. As he walked, he noticed the beginnings of an extraordinary sunset. "There was just the right kind of clouds and the sky was starting to burn and the bare trees were black as soot against it."

Upon arrival at his packed classroom, Buechner had an inspiration, and he made time for it. Departing from his lesson plan, he switched off the lights, and everything seemed to disappear except the sunset's splendor, lighting up the windows. "There it was—the entire sky on fire by then, like the end of the world or the beginning of it."

For the next twenty minutes, no one in the room said a word. No one did anything at all but gaze. The greatest thing about the experience was the *un-busyness of it,* Buechner said.[7] The students were simply spellbound by the wondrous, even holy sight, and they seemed to feel bound together by their common witness. Surely, this was gift time.

How impoverished we would be if we didn't take the time to notice these gifts of God when they come to us.

Biblical Presence

In cities, we are good at the business of busyness and haste, and we might even consider time for God a luxury. The lives of the saints, who were often very active and busy people, stand in counterweight to this belief. So do the most important figures in Scripture.

David, from the time he was a shepherd to the time he was a king, was a busy man who sometimes made serious mistakes. Occasionally, he followed the impulse of the moment, as when he coveted Bathsheba, another man's wife (see 2 Samuel 11–12). But David always returned to God in repentance and praise. And, as an active man and monarch, he composed psalms of such lasting beauty, many of us still turn to them every day and, in corporate worship, every week.

Although his patience was sometimes sorely tried, Moses was constantly active in leading the people of Israel out of bondage and through the desert. And yet Moses never said he was too busy to commune with God. In fact, Moses wanted more of God and asked to see the Shekinah of the Lord: God's glory (Exodus 33:18–23). God granted this request to his servant, and the face of Moses was radiant after this encounter with his Lord (34:29–30).

In the gospels, we see that Jesus was almost constantly busy: healing, teaching, feeding, interacting with a wide range of people, from tax collectors to publicans to Pharisees, the righteous of their day. We have noted, however, that Jesus kept a pattern of alternation—a balance between cycles of intense activity and equally intense times of prayer.

Jesus also cautions Martha, the sister of his friend Lazarus, against busyness at the expense of prayerful contemplation. While her sister Mary sat at Jesus's feet, "Martha was cumbered about much serving, and came to him, and said, Lord, dost thou not care that my sister hath left me to serve alone? bid her therefore that she help me. And Jesus answered and said unto her, Martha, Martha, thou art careful and troubled about many things: But one thing is needful: and Mary hath chosen that good part, which shall not be taken away from her" (Luke 10:40–42).

Later Jesus invites three of His disciples to a quiet mountaintop, where He shows them His own glory: the Transfiguration. It is arguable that the only one of Jesus's disciples who seems too busy with worldly matters is Judas Iscariot. In any case, the disciples did not tell Jesus they were too busy to visit the mountain with their Master.

But we can't always pause on a mountaintop in our fast-paced lives. A friend finds that she doesn't need constant mountaintop experiences. A spiritual director and committed Christian, she makes time for God as she sits in a bus, a subway car, or gridlock traffic. Because her expectations are realistic, my friend doesn't limit her spirituality to specific locales or situations. She watches people, and even in the fast-striding pedestrian she catches a glimpse of the Holy Spirit moving among us.

I have learned a lot from this friend. Today, on my way to meet her, I prayed in a taxi caught in crosstown traffic. I might have used that time to fret. Instead I found twenty minutes of God-centered time on the cracked leather seat of a yellow cab.

Poised to Pause

Frank Laubach, an evangelical missionary, was active throughout his life in the service of others. Called the "Apostle of Literacy," Laubach founded programs that involved millions of people worldwide and was a pioneer in the adult literacy movement, his work taking him to Africa and the Philippines well before the term *global village* existed.

As busy as he was, though, Laubach practiced the presence of God constantly and believed that each of us could do the same. He felt that we are called to ceaseless prayer, as urged by the apostle Paul; Laubach's prayer life was an experience of joy, not duty, lived out amid an active schedule. He writes of turning his mind every hour, "moment by moment to God," and by doing so, feeling "the millions at looms and lathes could make the hours glorious."[8]

For many of us in cities, this is far from easy.

"Inevitably," writes Claudia Horwitz, "when you start thinking about developing a spiritual practice, barriers will surface. The most common revolve around time, and our perception of how little of it we have."[9]

We don't have to be missionaries like Frank Laubach to accomplish this.

I know that many busy people set aside several times a day for prayer, despite the pressure of their schedules. I've managed to do it too. I find that short, repeated prayers can run through my head like music. If I try, I also find that I can set aside at least one concentrated period a day to focus on God for about twenty minutes—sort of like some people who set aside time for exercise or piano lessons.

I find that if I schedule my "centering time," it happens. I like to offer each day to God as I wake in the morning and to offer the night hours in the same way. My prayers are not elaborate or poetic, but they are genuine. They are sometimes inconsistent. I've grown used to beginning all over again…and again…and again.

Emilie Griffin refers to a prayer which illustrates "a good way to pray the ordinary." The prayer was written by the renowned theologian Karl Rahner and is called "God of My Daily Routine." Rahner's prayer, notes Griffin, "is ideal for those of us who feel hemmed in by a thousand daily responsibilities. How easy it is to suppose that God is far off, rather right in the middle of things with us."[10] And, I might add, how much more convenient. Perhaps some of us do not want God to be that near—with us, in all our foibles, in closeup.

Others, however, long for such nearness.

"My soul," writes Rahner, "has become a huge warehouse where day after day the trucks unload their crates without any plan or discrimination, to be piled helter-skelter in every available corner and cranny, until it is crammed full from top to bottom with the trite, the commonplace, the insignificant, the routine." And this, from one of the greatest theologians of our age. Rahner feels beset by "empty talk and pointless activity, idle curiosity and pretensions of importance that…roll forward in a never-ending stream."[11]

Most of us can identify with these sentiments. Rahner takes them several steps further—and in these steps, you and I can follow: "I must learn to have both 'every day' and Your day in the same exercise. In devoting myself to the works of this world, I must learn to give myself to You.… In You, all that has been scattered is reunited: in Your Love all the diffusion of the day's chores comes home again to the evening of Your unity."[12]

Offering the Heart

If we think of prayer as a technique, like breathing exercises, we miss the undergirding reason for praying at all. The spiritual writers of all eras tell us that prayer, fundamentally, is a matter of *love,* not a recipe to be accomplished as efficiently and quickly as possible.

Prayer, in the midst of ordinary hectic days, "calls for a certain attitude, offering of the heart to God in our simplest activities," writes Emilie Griffin in *Doors into Prayer.* "This inner disposition lets us receive God's blessing in and through our work. We may become conscious of God's love and mercy in surprising ways."[13]

Today, as I crossed a street, I moved faster to catch the green light. I was feeling scattered, not centered or prayerful. A three-way conversation from lunch was on my mind; at the same time, I felt pressured to get home and return a phone call. A woman was hurrying in my direction and did not step out of the way. Then, suddenly, she put out her arms to me for an embrace. Only then did I recognize her: she is my upstairs neighbor. And there, for a moment, she reminded me of God's grace— finding us, seeking us out, as she and I both walked hastily in opposite directions on a busy city avenue.

A sense of God's grace isn't always linked with a spectacular dawn or radiant sunset that makes us aware of the Holy in the ordinary. Often our closest moments with God are personal, ineffable, and totally devoid of special effects, as was my meeting with my neighbor in the harsh noon light of a winter's day.

"Another way prayer begins is in wonder," writes Emilie Griffin. "From early childhood we have a sense of the sacred but don't know to give it a name. I remember, at about age three, being amazed by sunlight filtering through my eye lashes.... All around me, when I was small there were experiences of wonder."

Griffin notes that C. S. Lewis felt a stab of childhood yearning beside a currant bush on a summer day. "Only after many years was he able to connect this experience with the presence of God. What he felt was sacredness and power. Such an experience of joy and praise may come in a flash, without warning. At last we guess that God is speaking to us with love."[14]

God in the Details

In the best-selling book *The Purpose-Driven Life,* pastor Rick Warren acknowledges that many might wonder why God would care about the details of our lives. However, Warren notes that "you can carry on a continuous open-ended conversation with [God] throughout your day, talking with him about whatever you are doing at the moment."[15]

God is passionate about His relationship with us, Warren asserts. "Every human activity, except sin, can be done for God's pleasure if you do it with an attitude of praise. You can wash dishes, repair a machine, sell a product, and raise a family for the glory of God."[16] It goes without saying that you can also craft a city life for God's glory as well.

In fact, many urban people find ways to pray in a manner that fits their pace. A busy midtown pastor runs every day; she finds that her running time blocks out distractions and offers her a good period for sustained prayer. She also finds "walking prayer" helpful; she can practice God's presence while she is in motion.

Another helpful discipline for her and many others is from the Eastern Orthodox *hesechast* tradition of ceaseless prayer, especially the silent recitation of what is known as the Jesus Prayer. In the ancient Orthodox tradition, ordinary people, as well as holy men, or startsy, keep this simple prayer running in their minds: "Lord Jesus Christ, Son of God, have mercy upon me."

This breath prayer, mentioned earlier, fits well with walking or running. Many other Christians say the Lord's Prayer or pray extemporaneously. Some Orthodox Jews listen to prayers on tape as they move through urban settings. A friend keeps favorite hymns in her mind as she goes about her errands in the city. She hums them. Their words surface as she waits for a bus or takes a number at the bakery. This practice gives her a sense of being companioned by God amid her mundane activities.

Again, I think of Brother Lawrence, practicing God's presence in the midst of mealtimes in his monastery's busy kitchen, with the pressure of feeding many people at once—and on time. This is not a new idea, we are reminded: practicing the presence of God in the midst of everyday rush and bustle. This is an idea that echoes throughout spiritual history.

Prayer by the Pros

I am blessed to have friends who are Carmelite nuns, women I've known for more than twenty-five years. These sisters are radiant, quietly aglow and humbly unaware of this. They are cloistered contemplatives, living in a beautiful monastery, as they call it, and they are certainly not as hurried as city dwellers. And while they show me a pace of life that makes me wistful, they have their times of pressure, moments when they must hurry.

I remember a time when I stayed for some days at this monastery and the extern sister was settling me into the guest room. As she did so, she completed one unfinished and prosaic task: hanging up a new shower curtain. I apologized for taking her away from her prayers.

"I *am* praying," she said, smiling and matter of fact.

How can this be? I wondered as I watched the sister's deft hands push plastic loops through a series of holes in a vinyl curtain, quickly, yet not in haste, just before joining her community for more formal noon prayer.

During this stay in the monastery guest room, I read the works of Dame Julian of Norwich, her particularly intense series of experiences called *Shewings*. Dame Julian, often sought for wise counsel, believed that we can never be separated from God. In a famous analogy to illustrate this union, she writes about a simple hazelnut—how we are like that small, seemingly insignificant object, but how God loves us and God holds us in being, how He dwells within each human soul, despite our weakness and sins and smallness.[17]

"Our soul is created to be God's dwelling place," she writes, "and the dwelling of our soul is God, who is uncreated." This is what my Carmelite hostess understood as she hung a shower curtain and considered herself to be in prayer. Nothing, she knew, could separate her from the presence of God.[18]

I try to carry the image of a shower curtain into my city life and let that image be a reminder to me of prayers in many forms.

During another stay at this particular monastery, during spiritual direction with a sister, I noticed a small insistent sound; it seemed to originate from the nun's cincture. To my surprise, the sound came from a small, discreet beeper. All the sisters had just gotten them in order to communicate, in times of need, across the far-flung grounds of the enclosure.

This time, there was a domestic emergency: the washing machine had overflowed. Some haste was needed. The sisters, however, do not seem to lose their centered focus, as so many of us do, even when in a hurry. I asked why.

"Practice," said the nun. "Practice. And love."

Staying Focused

Practice. And love. Every day those words help me to set aside at least one period of quiet time for centering prayer, where the focus is not on myself but on God. I use a prayer-word for God, as suggested by M. Basil Pennington, the noted spiritual guide and proponent of centering prayer.[19] I admit freely that it is often difficult for me to slow down and make room for this special time.

Yesterday, a day of many interruptions, distractions, and fragmented hours, I missed my twenty-minute period of quiet time with God, and I was aware of its absence. I realized that this miniretreat has become a deep spiritual well on which I draw. It's not duty, not a technique, but a time of restoration and relationship.

In his fine, small book *Making Room for God,* Melvyn Matthews writes that each person has within them "a great deal of inner space. In order to be whole, each of us has to recognize and to welcome this inner space and accept it as the most wonderful gift.... It is also the place of encounter with God."[20]

It's so often difficult for us to take time for contemplation. And yet, it's not only the monk or the nun who manages it. Many working people schedule periods of prayer on their calendars. Pennington suggests a twenty-minute interval, and in the introduction to his book *Centered Living,* we discover that Pennington has practiced centering in many places, including the corner of a hotel lobby.[21]

"Take a breath," we often say.

"Take a time-out."

It can be as simple as that, if we have the intention. I find time-outs helpful throughout the day. Interior monologues, even if they are offered up and directed to God, can sometimes be more oriented to ourselves rather than the Holy One. Of course, it's well and good to bring our needs to God; all spiritual writers encourage petitionary and discursive prayer.

The problem arises, perhaps, when we find our focus shifting away from God. This happens to me frequently. I've learned to accept breaks in my concentration. What kinds of breaks? The big-voiced horn of a giant truck outside. A mental reminder of someone I must call. A worry. Pressure. Deadlines. Running for the bus. But I've come to be patient with myself—after all, I believe that God is even more patient with me than I can imagine. When I can remain centered on God, I emerge from the silence with a different perspective. I feel quiet inside, and I'm reminded that I'm never alone.

How do we focus on another? Perhaps we are like the subject of an old joke about a person in "conversation" with a friend. This conversation becomes a monologue, and a long one. The friend listens patiently; at last, the speaker pauses and says, "But enough about me. I want to hear *you* talk about me."

How easy it is for us all to slip into this attitude, without devoting some time to God, who is always present with us, even in our haste.

Making Haste

Haste may take many forms for us in a fast-paced urban life; it's not only physical movement that goes quickly. Information comes at us so quickly as well—through faxes and cell phones, BlackBerries and instant messages, and iPhones that do it all. Time management and time coaching have become giant enterprises.

If we get frustrated with dial-up on the Internet, how much more frustrated we may become with God, who rarely contacts us at the speed of instant messaging?

Philosopher Blaise Pascal understood this four centuries ago. He was no stranger to urban society's diversions. However, he learned they had limitations. In his *Pensées,* he wrote, "We never keep to the present. We recall the past: we anticipate the future as if we found it too slow in coming and were trying to hurry it up, or we recall the past as if to stay its too rapid flight."[22]

I've often been reminded that things happen according to God's timing, not our own. And this age-old wisdom may frustrate us all the more today, especially in cities, where bicycle messengers cut in front of us and faxes hum all over the urban landscape. God's time is something that we cannot control. And yet, in the practice of waiting on the Lord, we may find a greater sense of peace and break the rush cycle.

Making Space

Many years ago, in a big city, I took an in-depth course on spirituality and prayer. At the start of each session, the teacher encouraged his students to use a few moments to get quiet and pay attention to our breathing, noting its movement, sensing it slow down as we grew more centered.

In one session, the teacher projected a beautiful icon on a screen before us. It was a representation of Christ's face: not stern, but compassionate, with eyes that seemed to search us. With the lights turned out, this face appeared to fill the room. There was nothing, it seemed, but that timeless gaze.

Our assignment was to center on this image for twenty minutes, letting ourselves realize that we were known by the Holy One in an intimate way, known and loved, no matter who we were or what we had done in our lives. This twenty-minute period of contemplation was, for me, a

MEASURE YOUR *Hurry-Sickness*

Give yourself five points for every question you answer yes and one point for every question you answer no.

_____ Do I feel compelled to do everything fast?

_____ Do I habitually rush wherever I'm going?

_____ Do I have difficulty waiting for results, answers, events?

_____ Do I make lists or plan to accomplish more things in a day than is truly possible?

_____ Do I find myself antsy and looking for escape when others are speaking to me?

_____ Do I cut off people on the road when driving or walking along city streets?

_____ Do I feel a sense of anger or frustration when others are ahead of me—in a line, on the road, walking?

_____ Do others tell me to slow down or stop or wait at least once a day?

_____ My Score

SCORE: If you end up with 32–40 points, you need to intentionally concentrate on ways to slow down or connect more deliberately with the world (and heavens) around you. If you score 24–28 points, you should be more conscious of your hurry-sickness and try centering prayer to ease your haste and increase your intimacy with others and God. If you rate 16–20 points, hurry-sickness may not be your main concern but something to be aware of. If you rate 8–12 points, you're managing haste and speed in the city fairly well, and you can help a more harried, hurried friend.

moving experience, although I did struggle at times to stay focused and centered. When my attention slipped away from the icon, I noticed that some of my classmates were in tears. Others were still, rapt, touched. And some could not sit through the twenty minutes.

Next to me, a man burst out of the room after a few moments, as if in flight, to smoke his pipe outside until the exercise was over.

I think many of us have that urge to resist intimate, focused time with God. Such focus does not fit our quick pace and may get on our nerves. It's not easy, either, to be reminded that *we* are not always in control. We're so used to pressing the keys, to making things happen and happen quickly, especially in cities.

But for those who write about the spiritual time-out, there is deep peace and joy in surrendering to God's presence. Throughout the ages Christians knew something that we may have forgotten. They knew, Melvyn Matthews writes, "that 'being before God' releases energy rather than diminishes it. 'Being before God' does not put some sort of damper on your true self.... Rather it enables you to know who you are and what this real self can do. It then sets you free to do it."[23]

I have found this to be true when I make time for God. As Thomas Kelly writes, "Voluntary or stated times of prayer merely join into and enhance the steady undercurrent of quiet worship that underlies the hours.... Through the shimmering light of Divine Presence, we look out upon the world, and in its turmoil, and its fitfulness, we may be given to respond, in some increased measure, in ways dimly suggestive of the Son of Man."[24]

For you and me, and for all who have gone before us, known and unknown, this kind of joy inspires deep gratitude. For each of us today, amid the haste of busy cities, we can discover prayer time in the hanging of a shower curtain—and in periods of quiet contemplation, each of us can reach the God who indwells us all.

My father was always in a hurry. "Got to make the light," he'd say halfway down the block as we approached an intersection, any intersection. He was perpetually early for everything. Traffic jams drove him to distraction. But at the bedsides of his patients, he was unhurried and fully present. In the middle of the night, he always picked up the phone and spoke at length with people in pain. He never rushed those who turned to him for help.

This made an indelible impression on me, his only daughter. As I look back now across the years, I see something shining in this doctor-patient relationship. In my mind, it will always model the infinite and loving time God makes for me, for you, for everyone living in speed-struck cities—cities where God always waits to meet us around every corner.

In thee, O LORD, do I put my trust; let me never be ashamed:
*   deliver me in thy righteousness.*
Bow down thine ear to me; deliver me speedily: be thou my strong
*   rock, for an house of defence to save me.*
For thou art my rock and my fortress; therefore for thy name's sake
*   lead me, and guide me. (Psalm 31:1–3)*

CURES FOR *Soulsickness* IN THE CITY

Stop: Read and Receive

1. How bad is my hurry-sickness? See the self-quiz on page 59.
2. What helps me to slow down to make time for God? Can I use imagery or music to do this? Can I allow myself more time to get where I must be and practice breath prayer on the way?
3. Do I feel impatient when I walk behind a slow pedestrian? Am I able to slow my own steps to walk in rhythm with that person's pace and so connect with a stranger?
4. Do I find that I am even in hurry mode when I go to a worship service? Can I allow more time for worship, coming early and using those extra moments to breathe deeply and prepare my spirit for the worship to come?

Yield: Reflect, Journal, or Discuss

5. What difficulties do I have keeping up with the fast pace of the city? What three ways have I felt overwhelmed or swept along by others on the sidewalk or in traffic? What three things can I do to maintain my own pace and make it prayerful?
6. When I sit in silence before God, how can I focus God's presence? Is there a word to help me focus? What phrases help?
7. How can I use breath prayer to slow down my pace? What prayer can I say internally, silently, in one breath as I move about the city?

8. What time of the day can I fast or abstain for an hour (or longer) from checking my e-mail or voice mail or from instant messaging? In those fasting times, what can I do to gently become mindful of God and His people?

Go: Experience and Engage

9. Practice keeping your mind on a prayer today without looking at your watch or clock.

10. Each morning this week, make time for God before your active day begins. At bedtime each evening, review the ways God has been working in your life through the day and week.

11. In a notebook, record your waking hours. Where do you see small gaps of time that you can use for brief but focused prayer? Make two or three appointments to be with God each week.

12. Use breathing and meditation to slow down. When you slow down your mind, practice giving that time to God.

FINDING GOD IN STRESS

The Gateway to Serenity

M y friend turned off her cell phone before we started lunch. Looking around the crowded restaurant, she noted how elusive peace is for so many city dwellers. Smart, compassionate, and savvy, she had been a banker for many years. Far ahead of retirement age, she's changed her lifestyle for more time with her husband, extensive travel, and enjoyment of her city's cultural oases.

People constantly ask her, "What do you do?" It's taken courage for her to say, "I'm not working right now."

She observed that there's often an awkward silence by way of response, and she noted how defined city people (commuters and residents alike) are by careers and the level of busyness, things that sadly become identity.

My friend's opted out of that and has no longing to go back to it. Even so, she still finds that busyness overtakes her. The moment she comes home, she admits, she throws down her coat and rushes to her computer to check e-mail, answer e-mail, and shop online. She wonders why she can't allow herself five or ten minutes to decompress or simply do nothing. "I have that time, and no message is really urgent," she reflects, puzzled and amused. "I need to be more aware of the moment."

She's certainly not alone. I marvel at how adept pedestrians are at text messaging, cell phoning, and checking BlackBerries—all the while crossing busy city streets, avoiding a taxi's sharp turn, dodging a bicycle messenger here, a pram there, a pedicab in between. Crossing a busy urban avenue even without a cell phone can be a complicated task.

City stress takes various forms: being overextended, overscheduled, overworked, pressed to impress, pressed for time, harried, hurried, hustled, hassled, harassed. Everyone wants something from us—and wants it yesterday.

This is not an exaggeration or a caricature. The stress of urban living is real: discussed, described, and deconstructed. It's defined by some as a sense of relentless pressure, by others as a state of constant tension, often pictured as a form of unstoppable motion—a treadmill, a rat race, or life in the fast lane.

Status Seduction

For most city dwellers, there's pressure simply to pay the bills and keep going. People depend on us; city life is expensive. The staffers in my building make long commutes to keep their shifts, and they never complain. A porter told me recently that he feels lucky to have a job, despite traffic and tension and tiring work.

There's also pressure to succeed materially, to keep up with the glamorous city lifestyle idealized in advertising and the media; failing to meet expectations increases stress and adds pressure to work harder, jump higher, and shine more splendidly still.

Some aspects of urban culture stimulate a desire to make it big city–style: get the bigger bonus, better wristwatch, the brighter smile, finer designer suit, more-polished decorator kitchen, most desirable table in the most exclusive restaurant—and a penthouse with a view of the metropolis, sparkling like a vast, glowing fiefdom, far below.

A former banker told me that the only billionaire she knows is unhappy and insecure. No matter what he does on Wall Street, there is always someone with a greater edge, more money, a bonus that trumps his. He's wealthier than the vast majority of the population, but in his particular fast lane, he's the slowest one. And so he has become a stressed-out person who lives large and spends most of his waking hours at work.

"Once we are ensnared in the habit of acquiring as a way to achieve happiness, it is difficult to break," writes Arthur Jeon. "No matter how much is actually purchased, if the dynamic is still locked in place, there is always more that is available, another high to attain and another person to outspend.... The final result is a feeling of separation and emptiness.... 'Is this all there is?'"[1]

Is it?

For many of us—*no.*

Urban Envy

I remember having "penthouse envy" for a while. But I would feel a strange emptiness after each visit to a new real estate listing. The lure of the penthouse, for me, was mostly to find a haven from the city, to be high enough to live beyond the noise, the crowds, the haste, the hassle. But I must confess that I had also succumbed to a certain kind of urban pressure: the need to have a desirable nest high above the city. There were small penthouses on the market—nothing ostentatious, just high enough to be a refuge.

One, I recall, was breathtaking: on the thirty-seventh floor with that touted urban feature "outdoor space" in the form of a narrow, wraparound terrace. I liked the prospect of the city twinkling at night—visible from three exposures. It reminded me of an advertisement of a glittering city I'd seen as a young girl. In that magazine ad, a man and a woman are toasting each other in front of a fabulous city view: the darkness, pricked with thousands of glimmering lights. Clearly, the product being sold didn't interest me at all, and the couple in the photo didn't interest me nearly as much as that dark, lit, atmospheric space beyond them, visible through the floor-to-ceiling windows.

It was some time before I realized that this penthouse view actually reminded me of something totally different: the interiors of St. Patrick's Cathedral and Chartres Cathedral, and all the cathedrals and churches I've loved—their dim naves flickering with the dance of innumerable votive lights. My mind and spirit seem to bend, to lean, to veer, inexorably, toward those places of the mind and heart.

After this realization, the seductive power went out of that penthouse, and all others, even the small, affordable ones. I realized that there was no refuge from the city in an aerie, however logical this seemed at first.

The solution to urban dwelling, for me, was to live smaller and lower and more simply and, most important, to come to terms with the city through a consistent prayerful spirituality. This would be a lasting way of life and didn't depend on the vagaries of co-op boards and monthly maintenance fees.

This is not something that is easily explicable to most real estate agents. This is not necessarily understandable in most big cities, where so many get what they want and still want more. And more. Still more.

The *New York Times* ran an editorial on the "Haves and Have Mores," which was widely discussed.[2] When the figures came out on CEOs' huge Christmas bonuses, the "Have Mores" were discussed again—and, downtown in every city, even as you read these words, there are people living high-stress, high-pressure lives, seven days a week, to get the dream of urban success and hold on to it with both hands. But as time passes, one wonders what the price is, emotionally and spiritually.

Busyness

"I am soooo busy."

"I am *so* very busy."

"I am so incredibly busy."

These are the opening lines of three e-mails I received on one day as I busied myself at the computer. Each sender, I'm sure, was too busy to pray. I know I was. And that was only one day, one typical Monday. By the end of the week I'd sent and received numerous e-mails with the word *busy* in them.

We are overbooked, overworked, overscheduled, overwhelmed. And city life tends to reinforce this pattern. Being busy can, in some circles, be seen as a sign of importance, popularity, and success. Where does prayer come in?

Rick Hamlin, a busy urban editor, finds openings for it. "There are spot prayers uttered at work between taking a telephone call, making a trip to the water cooler, and wrestling with icons on the computer," he writes. "Prayers I say in bed at night when I can't get to sleep because of worries about friends, or work, or family. And then there are songs that are prayers lingering in my head."[3]

I too find that spot prayer and prayerful songs help me get through stressful days. These times are like deep breaths for me and a reminder that God is larger than any stress.

"From birth we have been learning the rules of self-reliance and we strain and struggle to achieve self-sufficiency," Bill Hybels explains in his book *Too Busy Not to Pray: Slowing Down to Be with God.* "Prayer flies in the face of these deep-seated values. It is an assault on human autonomy, an indictment of independent living. To people in the fast lane, determined to make it on their own, prayer is an embarrassing interruption."[4]

In this fast lane, the act of turning to God at all may seem like an embarrassing interruption. By doing so, you admit that you can't go it entirely alone. You may feel that if you need to make time for God, you're weak, deficient, unable to cut it, ace it, or slam dunk it all by yourself.

"And yet somewhere, someplace, probably all of us reach the point of falling to our knees," Hybels affirms, "bowing our heads, fixing our attention on God and praying."

Dad's Turn

I understand this thinking. My father, a dedicated atheist, held all those opinions through most of his life. He was a successful surgeon, though never successful enough in his own eyes. He worked harder than anyone I've ever known, and he worked long hours; he even made house calls at night.

Medicine was my father's religion, his life, and I heard his endless, private scorn for religious people of any faith. At the same time, he was unusually compassionate to the poor and friendless and pained—and to these he ministered with what C. S. Lewis calls "Gift Love": graced, unconditional love, rather than "Need Love."[5]

So perhaps it is not surprising that my father became spiritual at the very end of his life. He had survived a serious heart attack, and he well knew his medical condition as well as his family's cardiac history. He spent a great deal of time alone in his favorite chair those last few months, between the first heart attack and the second, fatal one. My father's spiritual journey was our secret. I was to tell no one. I still hesitate, after all these years.

The tall terror of my childhood, my father had been an imposing man. It was only in those last months that the power seemed to go out of him as he sat and thought about his life. Once, on a visit, I apologized for being too busy to come sooner. We were alone in the elegant living room, and my father looked into my eyes.

I remember the silence between us; I could hear the doorman whistle for a taxi far below in the city street. "It's good to be busy, Cookie," he said finally, using his nickname for me from when I was a child. "But not too busy. I was…too busy."

I stared at him, and that was when I noticed the books in his lap. One was a Bible. I was stunned; I didn't think he owned one. It was open to the gospel of Luke, and it was well thumbed. I stared in amazement; my father smiled.

My eyes jumped to the other book on his lap: *Spoon River Anthology* by Edgar Lee Masters, a famous collection of epitaph-like poems, delivered as if from a midwestern town's graveyard. My father had turned down a page in this book, which he now opened. He glanced up, smiled again, and read to me the poem epitaph that he had almost memorized:

I who lie here was the village atheist,
Talkative, contentious, versed in arguments

Of the infidels.
But through a long sickness…
I read the *Upanishads* and the poetry of Jesus.
And they lighted a torch of hope and intuition
And desire which the Shadow,
Leading me swiftly through the canyons of darkness,
Could not extinguish.[6]

My father told me that he "very definitely" was not experiencing "death-bed religion," which he had seen many times as a doctor. He told me that he was not afraid of dying. He told me that he had regrets, many regrets. Some are too personal to repeat here. There was a long pause. And then my father confessed that for years he had been reading about Jesus. It began this way: as a physician, my father had been curious about the Crucifixion; he had pored over Jim Bishop's *The Day Christ Died.* The book had drawn him; he had read it again and again.

He had gone on to read what Jesus had said during His life. The modern, big-city doctor had been mesmerized by the gospels' healing stories. The atheist had been struck to the core by the passion of Jesus to minister to the sick, the broken, the poor.

"Daddy," I remember saying just the one word. I had not called him that in a long time.

"All these years," he confided, "I was too busy to see it. To see clearly." He paused again. "Too proud to let it in. I thought believing wasn't for smart people. I was wrong…" He trailed off and reached for my hand.

Your CPA Is Required

The last thing I saw in my father's eyes was peace. I had never seen that in his gaze before, and I had been looking into his eyes for decades. When you think about it, peace is not evident in many a gaze, especially in our lives of urban busyness.

In cities, we are passionate about multitasking. I have learned a new name for the kind of awareness this breeds: CPA, or continuous partial attention. In the March 27, 2006, issue of *Newsweek,* Steven Levy wrote an article about a Microsoft executive who was speaking at a conference on this very subject.

"She couldn't have picked a more perfect audience," writes Levy. "During the presentations [at the conference], the faces of at least half the crowd were lit with the spooky reflection of the laptops open before them. Those without computers would periodically bow their heads to the palmtop shrine of the BlackBerry. Every speaker was competing with the distractions of e-mail, instant messaging, Web surfing, online bill paying, blogging, and an Internet chat 'back channel' where the conferees supplied snarky commentary on the speakers."[7]

Why do we do this? Do we cram our schedules so tightly, with so many distractions, because we are avoiding time to think? to face ourselves? to face into life's spiritual dimension? Perhaps the answer is different for each person. But each one of us can, if we choose, pare down our busyness to make time for God…if we so desire.

I find it helps to make a list in two columns: Essentials and Nonessentials. It surprises me how many nonessentials there are and how many opportunities there are for pauses, for prayer, for practicing the presence of God.

"I need a lot of pauses," said Joy Lewis, the beloved wife of C. S. Lewis, as she recovered from an illness. A woman of deep faith, she may have meant this on many levels.

She speaks for me—and for many.

Be Still and Know

The everyday prayers of monks "used to be part of our traditional society, before we got too busy," notes Dr. Herbert Benson. "The mental health, the quietude, the ability to deal with stress that the monks have can be captured by us in our regular busy lives."

We do not make space for God because it is good for our health, of course, but many people remind us that "it is a terrible error to believe that we don't have time for this." The very features of pausing to practice

God's presence, of stopping for prayer, "can come to sustain us and protect us."[8]

Benson goes on to suggest that we can learn to be still, right where we are, and be "present to the present moment...and to God and others." We have to "slow down to catch up with ourselves," Benson suggests.

Another friend would like to slow down to catch up with herself. We discussed the process of taking a few minutes before computer time, before dinnertime, before each task for quiet time with God. This friend was used to rushing from the front door directly to her e-mail. She realized that she might come to look forward to such slowing down.

This isn't just an artistic flight of fancy, but a deep insight. We may be avoiding such moments...or longer periods of time, when we transcend the self and feel united with the Holy One.

"As the hart panteth after the water brooks," writes the psalmist, "so panteth my soul after thee, O God" (Psalm 42:1). And the One who knows us best and loves us most says, "Be still, and know that I am God" (46:10).

These experiences are not reserved for special people—they are available to us all, if we can and will make the time.

"Prayer," writes an anonymous author, "is so simple. It is like quietly opening a door and slipping into the very presence of God. There, in the stillness, we listen to His voice.... Just to be there in His presence is prayer."

Making Time

I know a man who has opened that door to simple prayer. "How do you hold on?" I once asked him.

He grinned, showing gaps between his teeth. "I pray a lot," he said.

Ben, weathered, in his forties, sits with his wife, straddling milk crates they have set up on a hectic urban avenue. Newly homeless, recently mugged, Ben watches the human parade rush by while his wife sleeps on his shoulder.

To most of us, they are invisible. To him, we are a stream that doesn't change much, he says. What does he see in our faces?

"Worry. Mostly it's worry. Planning, you see that too. Wheels turning. Then there's this way people have, the ones on cells [phones], they're looking in, not out." He sees people absorbed in their own problems, people overtaken by pressure.

He doesn't mention peace, I notice. I wait. That word doesn't come.

"Peace?" a Realtor friend exclaimed when I told her of the conversation with Ben. She doesn't have much time for peace. She has a full-time job in the city, a suburban renovation, a young daughter, and a busy BlackBerry and cell phone. During the last year, she's been sick too often and begun to think seriously: *Is my health worth all this? How can I find quiet time in my stressful days for the spiritual dimension?*

This friend's time to herself is an hour's train commute, when she can sit alone and reflect. Lately, she's also begun going back to church. In the quiet there, she says that she looks down the pew and feels filled with gratitude for her family. And in that gratitude to God is a sense of worshipful peace. It's a quiet awakening.

"We are always completely, and therefore equally, known to God," C. S. Lewis said. "That is our destiny.… The door in God that opens is the door he knocks at."[9]

I try to think about God when I stand before doors of any kind and attempt to remember that Jesus told us to ask, to knock (see Matthew 7:7). In order to do that, we must pause and readjust our speed.

"I don't know you, of course," writes Susie Davis in *The Time of Your Life: Finding God's Rest in Your Busy Schedule.* "I don't know if your busyness is a cover for negative feelings such as guilt, anger, sadness, or inadequacy. And I certainly can't say whether you're trying to close your ears to God. But I've seen it happen enough, even in my own life, that I have to raise the possibility.… Could it be that you are allowing busyness to buffer you from facing some uncomfortable truth about your life or, more important, from hearing the voice of God?"[10]

These questions would make many of us squirm. I've known people who are so well defended that they wouldn't tolerate such queries. But these are important questions for us to ask ourselves, especially amid stressful city life. It's too bad we opt to let busyness define us, or as Davis says,

"We pack our calendars with appointments and entertainments, with importance and ambition, with need-to-dos and want-to-dos. Busyness even becomes a badge of honor—we can't wait to tell somebody, *anybody*, how incredibly busy we are."[11]

Do you engage in busyness to signify importance, to give you the feeling that you're needed, that you're prospering? There's a perception that those who aren't busy are somehow less valuable, less central, less vital.

It takes effort to resist this kind of thinking. It's worth a reminder, Davis says, that prayer time can change this perspective, and prayer is priceless. "God has so much more for you. He has promised meaning in even the most despairing circumstances. He can calm your restless heart. He can balance your days. He wants to be the meaning in your life, the center of your schedule. And He can help you manage your schedule with healthy balance. He can help you love your life again."[12]

God waits for us. Sometimes it takes a tragedy or an illness or a reversal to make us realize that. But it needn't, because God waits. Like the father in the parable of the prodigal son, God waits to welcome us home with an embrace after, Davis says, "you find the courage to stop running. He will actually run to you, if you acknowledge your need of His help. He not only feels compassion for you—he longs for your return.... The road home is as simple as an acknowledgment that all the busyness in your life does not come close to supplying your needs the way God does."[13]

I believe that this is what my father finally accepted at the end of his life. A dear friend of mine also experienced a change in her own highly intellectual father—an atheist, a professor, then a convert.

Both fathers had lacked respect for people who needed God in their lives; they often commented that people of faith turned to religion because they needed a crutch, a drug, magic. But time showed otherwise.

"I wish there was more time," my father said to me during our revelatory conversation. "Now that I know. Every day, every week, I wish there was more time."

Stress Hits Home

It has finally happened.

Busyness has got the best of me.

Yesterday I was "too busy to pray" except in the most perfunctory way, while slicing fruit for breakfast and dinner, I confess. At no time did I pause to give God my undivided attention, neglecting my usual periods of centering prayer.

Instead, I was e-mailing, preparing for class, teaching class, correcting papers, responding to students, scurrying about the city, ordering groceries… You probably know how that litany goes. I should have awakened especially early, in anticipation of a harried day, to make time for prayer. Without that island of quiet with God, my whole day is thrown off for me.

What do you do if you're nonstop busy with a swarm of tasks that aren't optional distractions, that must be done now?

Today, as I pondered this, I turned first to Brother Lawrence and then Frank Laubach—two very different people: a Catholic and a Protestant, separated by three hundred years but joined forever in their devotion and closeness to God. They were highly active people who were prayerfully attentive to the Holy. Lawrence and Laubach, dedicated to "being before God," have a great deal to offer our stressed-out urban lives.

Brother Lawrence was a seventeenth-century Carmelite monk who worked most of his vowed life in his monastery's busy kitchen. Whether he was in chapel or in the kitchen, he felt equally near to God, by offering up all his work with constant mindfulness to the Holy, he said in his classic book *The Practice of the Presence of God.* Amid the clatter of his pots and pans, and the pressure of precise mealtimes for a multitude, this humble monk kept his mind fixed on God's presence with him. Every task Brother Lawrence did was performed "before God." He insisted that to be consistently aware of God's presence, it is necessary to form the habit of continually talking with Him throughout the day.

To think you must abandon conversation with God in order to deal with the world is wrong, Lawrence affirmed. In God's presence, he said, "We will derive a great joy in being His."[14]

Brother Lawrence encourages us to habitually cultivate the practice of the presence of God. At first, he admits, he himself had difficulty with the building of this habit, but it grew easier, and as it did so, his constant sense of God's presence brought the monk delight.[15]

It seems that those who practice the presence share this sense of delight. The practice is not a duty nor a burden but a source of quiet joy. Brother Lawrence was known for the happiness and radiance of his countenance.

Missionary Frank Laubach, Brother Lawrence's modern counterpart and also a happy man, would have agreed with him. "In the chinks of time between the things we find ourselves obliged to do," Laubach wrote, "there are the moments when our minds ask: 'What next?' In these chinks of time, ask Him: 'Lord, think Thy thoughts in my mind. What is on Thy mind for me to do now?' When we ask Christ, 'What next?' we tune in and give Him a chance to pour His ideas through our enkindled imagination. If we persist, it becomes a habit."[16]

I will try to remember these two soul mates, Lawrence and Laubach, as I go into my next overloaded day, and I will also carve out more focused, quiet centering-prayer time, first thing in the morning and also in the evening, as I used to do.

I cannot use the familiar excuse, "I'm too tired." My great friend and mentor, the late Thomas P. Gavigan, SJ, passed along a personal memory that stays with me. His own father was an Irish immigrant who worked long hours in a factory so that his children could have an education.

My mentor remembers finding his father on his knees before his bed at night, often with his head resting on the mattress, saying his prayers after a hard day's work. For him, said his son, this was important time, a kind of brief Sabbath time at the end of every day.

On Sunday, all day, the Sabbath was faithfully, fully, and happily observed. Father Gavigan's hardworking parents lived in a Pennsylvania city at a time in the last century when shops were closed on Sundays and commerce did not go on 24/7. Perhaps we are having less Sabbath time in cities and large towns and perhaps that adds to our stress—as well as a loss of time to renew ourselves with God.

Making Sabbath Time

"I don't know about you," an Oregon pastor said recently, "but for me the concept of a Sabbath gets challenged all the time by our 24/7 world. It is rare anymore that stores will be closed any day of the week, let alone the Sabbath. Just what would we do if our cell phone capability were to be cut off for a whole day each week? I certainly struggle with this.… And I know I am not alone in this."[17]

I think that most of us, in urban settings, struggle to create Sabbath time, once a week and even once (or more often) a day. Such time-outs for God are crucial to my entire orientation to life—especially life in the big city.

I confess that I am old enough to remember when major cities would fall silent on Sundays and a sweet hush would fold down over the tall buildings. The world seemed to pause, synchronized with rhythms larger than its own. There would be the chime of church bells. God was bigger than the city, those days, in my childhood.

A Chapel in the Pines

This was accentuated for me in childhood summers, when I went to camp in Maine. Sunday was the one day we did not have activities. Instead, we had a contemplative service in an outdoor chapel, surrounded by a grove of pine trees.

I remember hearing Saint Paul's famous words on love (see 1 Corinthians 13) read into the stillness there, punctuated by the breeze in the pines. We sang hymns and psalms, while the lake beyond us danced in the light. I suppose that every Sunday of my city life, a part of my spirit revisits that time.

This camp, however, didn't limit Sabbath time to Sundays. At least once a week, in the early evening, we were invited into a time of private creative writing and contemplation on the beach by the lake. There were times for pauses throughout each day. Before every meal, there was a moment of silence and a sung grace. I still remember the words filling the simple, raftered dining hall and our girlish voices rising in traditional table graces.

I also remember the way our cabin lights were swiftly turned off at 9 p.m. for a few moments and how during this time "Taps" was played and a prayer was said.

I try to remember that experience now, so many years later. And I long for those simple pauses for God.

I started at this camp when I was nine years old and continued there until I was fifteen. There I learned some of the sustained rhythms of a spiritual life balanced with activity, and I have brought that time, that place, that rhythm with me into my urban existence. To this day, if I catch the scent of pine or see a birch tree, I am immediately transported back to a sense of reverence and grace; a space for God opens up in my daily routine. All I have to do, really, is close my eyes and I am there.

Sabbath Grace

Instead of moving to the Maine woods, however, I try to keep that Sabbath reverence I learned there. I fail often. Sabbath keeping is a challenge for all of us in metropolitan areas, especially where stores and entertainments and restaurants are open 24/7 and a high level of stimuli, without pause, comes at us.

However, a seasoned Lutheran pastor observes that urban people who come to worship are very intentional and motivated about Sabbath time. In a city, there is so much competing for our attention—and yet so many city dwellers do choose to make time, exclusively, for God.

In his classic book *Sabbath Time,* Tilden Edwards sees Sabbath keeping not only as a day of rest but as a time of renewal, reconnection, and hope. It can bring us a break from the weekday pressures and distractions, but it can also open up space for the Holy. Edwards, a Protestant, was deeply influenced by time spent with an Orthodox Jewish community and its way of celebrating the Sabbath with devotion, attentiveness, and joy.

Corporate worship, for Edwards, does not stand alone in our greater focus on God, whenever we observe the Sabbath. "Corporate worship," he writes, "to be its intended self, needs to be surrounded by a protective time zone, a time of preparation and reflection, of quiet openness with nothing to do except appreciate the presence of God in the smallest random thing in and around us."[18]

"If this is done," Edwards continues, "then corporate worship is more likely to become a radiant crystal whose facets catch up all of life in God's light, placed in the midst of a velvet Sabbath bed that sets it off. Without such surrounding Sabbath time, worship will more likely resemble an opaque rock that reveals nothing of life's giftedness and integrity of God, only our rushed anxiety."[19]

As a city person, I think that I might feel less stressed if I created more Sabbath time for myself; Sabbath for me means corporate worship and often a visit to a place of peace. Sometimes it's a garden, sometimes a certain museum's display of medieval Christian art. I try to practice centering prayer for a longer period on the Sabbath than I do during the week, but this isn't easy to live out. There's so much to do in a city 24/7.

What helps is an intention to remain especially open to God's presence on Sundays, and then it's easier for me to be reverently attentive during the week.

In the end, it's not about discipline, this soulfulness in the city. It's about remembering who loves me and knows me best. I like to go to a fountain in a park, in particular the Bethesda Fountain in Central Park, which centers around an angel. This fountain commemorates a pool where Jesus healed a paralytic. I like to think of God's presence as I watch this angel of the waters, and I like to imagine Christ's healing hand reaching out to me.

A Radical Act

What does Sabbath keeping do for you? How has it changed your life?

Keeping the Sabbath is "a radical act of resistance," Rebecca Parker observes. "It is an act of saying no to the message that tells us to fill the emptiness in our lives by consuming more.... When we decide to keep the Sabbath and not consume for one day in seven, we take a degree of control back in our lives."[20]

But it's up to each one of us to decide how to take time out of ordinary time and open up a space for God. Only we can know what will call us away from all the things that pressure us toward a place where we truly sense that we are in God's presence. Nor does this "Sabbath time" have to be consigned, and confined, to one day in seven.[21]

In *Sabbath Keeping,* Lynne M. Baab explores many ways of taking that pause for God. She attends corporate worship on Sunday and lets her Sabbath continue on Mondays. "The Sabbath has been a great gift to me," she writes, "by slowing me down and inciting me to experience God's rest—and not just analyze it. Jesus said to his disciples 'come to me, all you that are weary and are carrying heavy burdens and I will give you rest...and I will give you rest.' (Matthew 11:28–29). I have received that gift of Christ in rest on the Sabbath."[22]

Baab says that she tries to discern which activities to cease from and which activities help her to see God's miracles more clearly. For her, an increased and intentional period of gratitude is part of her Sabbath keeping.[23]

For many, ritual is important here. Often people mark the Sabbath with a meal or with special foods. If I light a candle and set out the icon I treasure, my stone from the holy island of Iona and my cross from Ireland, I'm preparing myself for a time set aside for God alone. For many people, a solitary walk has the same effect, and certain walks accommodate themselves to breath prayer.

Sabbath Rhythms

Many city dwellers feel the need to put aside a day for worship and practicing the joy of the presence of God. A Midtown pastor recently commented that urban Sabbath keepers seem especially intentional about their worship time because a city provides so many other options and distractions. But for all of us stressed urban people, the Sabbath need not end with the sundown of a particular day.

Perhaps if you can integrate Sabbath time in smaller amounts into every day, you'll be able to readjust your rhythms to the Holy One more easily.

Wayne Muller writes eloquently: "In the relentless busyness of modern life, we have lost the rhythm between work and rest. All life requires a rhythm of rest. There is a rhythm in our waking activity and the body's need for sleep. There is a rhythm in the way day dissolves into night and night into morning.... There is a tidal rhythm, a deep, eternal conversation between the land and the great sea. In our bodies, the heart perceptibly rests after each life-giving beat."[24]

Muller believes that we have lost this natural sense of rhythm, and I think this is particularly true in cities, where the earth is covered with concrete and the signs of the changing seasons are fewer. Observing the rhythm of Sabbath, each day and each week, helps us to align ourselves again with the rhythms that God created for us and for our time with the Holy.

Biblical Sabbath Keeping

Some form of Sabbath keeping has existed in many religious systems. The book of Nehemiah delineates Sabbath observance for the Hebrew people after their exile in Babylon (see Nehemiah 13:15–22). The prohibitions and restrictions were designed to facilitate concentration on God's presence and to welcome it with joy.

Jesus, of course, observed the Sabbath, as did His followers. In the gospel of Luke, we see Jesus reading from the holy writings on the Sabbath in Nazareth's synagogue where He worshiped. However, He emphasized that "the sabbath was made for man, and not man for the sabbath" (Mark 2:27). In accordance with this statement, Jesus healed the infirm on the Sabbath.

I wonder how often I stop to think about acts that glorify God. I wonder how many times I don't cease and desist from work and hurried behavior so that I can have more time for God, not just on the Sabbath but throughout the week. It's possible to create Sabbath time every day, I have realized, if I try, even if it's only for a few minutes. One way that I can do this is to light a candle at my desk and focus on the flame. I think of the fire of the Holy Spirit touching me and my work area.

Suddenly this time feels more important than anything else, and this can happen on a blue Monday or a "Thank God it's Friday."

Some days, I must admit, my candle is not lit, however. Those days I think about why anyone would resist a mini-Sabbath. Perhaps we believe that making time for God is akin to the experience of waiting, and some-times it is, but who likes to wait? Or perhaps we don't want God quite that present, quite that close, quite that often.

"Our culture invariably supposes that action and accomplishment are better than rest, that doing something—anything—is better than doing nothing," observes Wayne Muller in *Sabbath*. "Because of our desire to succeed…we do not rest. Because we do not rest, we lose our way. We miss the compass points that would show us where to go, we bypass the nour-ishment that would give us succor. We miss the quiet that would give us wisdom. We miss the joy and love born of effortless delight."[25]

Wise people have always known this. "If thou…call the sabbath a delight," wrote the prophet Isaiah, "then shalt thou delight thyself in the LORD; and I will cause thee to ride upon the high places of the earth" (58:13–14). And in Ecclesiastes, it is written: "Better is a handful with quietness, than both the hands full with travail and vexation of spirit" (4:6).

In the end, we're guided by God's rhythms, right down to the very pattern of our breathing, sleeping, talking, and listening. If we look, we will come to see "chinks of time," in the words of Frank Laubach, when God's loving nature will draw us back into the rhythm of holy joy. If we find one Sabbath chink, we're certain to find another, and another, until each of our days is dappled with God's light.[26]

God is our refuge and strength, a very present help in trouble.
Therefore will not we fear, though the earth be removed, and
though the mountains be carried into the midst of the sea;...
There is a river, the streams whereof shall make glad the city of
God, the holy place of the tabernacles of the most High.
God is in the midst of her; she shall not be moved: God shall help
her, and that right early. (Psalm 46:1–2, 4–5)

CURES FOR *Soulsickness*
IN THE CITY

Stop: Read and Receive

1. When do you feel that urban bustle and busyness have invaded your soul? Do you experience yourself as over-scheduled, overworked, and caught in the rat race or the fast lane? Do you find yourself too busy to pray?

2. How are you energized by keeping very busy? Do you ever wonder if you have to be busy to an extreme degree? When you look frankly within, would you find that busyness is a way to avoid the spiritual dimension of life?

3. You're aware that too much pressure and stress have negative effects on your physical health. Stop right now to inventory your spiritual health: what does stress do to your relationship with God and with others, regarding spiritual connection?

4. What scheduled "appointments" have you ever made with God, as some businesspeople and pastors do? Would you be willing to pencil in an appointment with God three times a week for a half hour? Could you move up that frequency to once a day? Map out a plan for yourself over the next two weeks. Note thoughts in your journal about the effects of such appointments in your life.

Yield: Reflect, Journal, or Discuss

5. Make a list, by priority, of what keeps you busy. What can you give up or where can you work in an appointment with God?

6. Have you ever experimented with the practice of offering up your work to God, as Brother Lawrence and Frank Laubach

did? Try this with one task you face today. Consider how you can practice the presence of God while you work and move about. How can that one task become like a prayer or an act of spiritual service? When you're deliberate about this, how do you feel? How is the work changed or not? Do you see effects of your work in this way upon others?

7. In the midst of busy city life, where can you find "chinks" between your appointed tasks, in Frank Laubach's words, for brief prayers and loving mindfulness of God's presence?

8. Do you see busyness as a sign of importance, popularity, and "having a life"? What do you believe about people who are less overtly busy? Examine your feelings and attitudes. When you're honest with yourself, do you feel that people who are less busy are losers, retired, or lazy?

Go: Experience and Engage

9. Journal about solitude. Notice if you fear it, desire it, or feel something in between.

10. Examine a typical day for you. Note the difference between things you *must* do and things you do just to keep busy. What are those things? How do you feel about them when you step back and look at them this way?

11. List what makes you feel burned out and what brings you peace of mind.

12. Today, as you walk or listen to music, say a prayer with the rhythm of your actions. How does this make you feel? Do you notice any changes around you?

Finding God in Distractions

The Gateway to Simplicity

Every Saturday when I was growing up in Manhattan, I would walk down Fifth Avenue and gaze into the windows of Tiffany and Cartier and Steuben Glass. Everything in those windows looked so beautiful to me: the glimmer of sculpted glass, the shine of polished gold, and the sparkle of finely crafted gems. Of course, as a teenager, I didn't have the wherewithal to purchase anything. But I don't remember longing to own Buccellati silver or Baccarat crystal "someday…"

I admired what I saw without feeling a need to have it.

I hasten to say this attitude was in no way due to my own virtue, but to something far more humbling, complicated, and disturbing. A daughter of privilege, I grew up in a household that was as dysfunctional as it was elegant. From an early age, I knew that having beautiful things didn't make for a happy home. I was fortunate in many ways, and to all outward appearances, I had it all. But Tiffany china and Baccarat crystal did not make my family into a functional, secure unit. I knew somehow, at an early age, that beautiful, expensive things never would change what really mattered nor would they feed my soul.

Many city dwellers, however, are entranced with the commercial plenty of an urban environment. Shop windows, boutiques, and stores of all kinds call to us—to have, get, buy. Can we lead spiritual lives without a certain amount of simplicity?

A Modern Parable

There is an old story told to me by my mentor, Father Gavigan, SJ. He didn't know the provenance of this parable, but that was less important than its meaning.

The story goes like this: A wise man showed a beautiful flower to three young novices. The first novice, who found the flower distracting from his ascetic spirituality, wanted to trample the blossom. The second novice found the flower spiritually uplifting and wanted to pluck it and take it with him. The third novice admired the flower's beauty, saw in it a feature of God's creation, and decided it was best to enjoy the flower in the earth where it could grow.

Father Gavigan never underlined the lesson in the parable—it was simply a story he recounted as I drove him to a communion call on an early spring afternoon in Washington DC. Daffodils were coming up, and the famous cherry blossoms had already appeared. He was thinking aloud about flowers and remembering, perhaps, his days as a novice master.

I thought of this story as I laid flowers on his grave; I often think of him and the many things he taught me, by word and by example, over a period of decades. My memories of him are particularly vivid when I confront the complexities of spirituality and city living.

Born in Scranton, Pennsylvania, Father Gavigan was a highly educated man with a deep, abiding spiritual sense. Once, as a young graduate student, I asked him if he might ever want to aspire to higher office, and he recoiled in horror.

"I just want to be a simple parish priest," he said. "I wouldn't want to clutter that up."

My mentor believed that simplicity was integral to the spiritual life. He eschewed all but the plainest wool suits and sometimes bought bus-boys' black jackets, in keeping with his vows of poverty. And yet, he respectfully served one of the wealthiest parishes in the city. He wasn't judgmental about wealth, but he knew that, for him, simplicity was most congruent with spirituality.

A Gavigan homily was usually on social justice; he felt that serving the poor was crucial to spiritual living. To this day, when I walk past the stores on Fifth Avenue, I think of Father Gavigan's parable about the novices and the flower.

Simple Ways

When many people move to cities, they must downsize or "downshift." This was my experience as I went from a house on a city's fringe to a series of apartments in the hearts of two major urban centers. It's amazing how much stuff we can accumulate, from kitchen drawers full of odd buttons and used matchbooks, to excess clothing, to sets of china (especially ironic for someone who doesn't cook). And why did I have nine oral thermometers and five broken watches?

A friend recently went through a similar experience and found the same duplication of objects, a plethora of books to give to libraries, and general kitchen clutter that surpassed her memory of purchasing those objects. *Why,* another friend wondered as she helped her mother relocate, *were there eight potato peelers in the cellar, along with ancient economy-sized jars of Heinz ketchup?*

We all found that the exercise of downsizing was revelatory, humbling, and had an inherent lesson in it about how attached we are to stuff.

But then detachment from material possessions has always been a part of spiritual struggle in every faith tradition.

Biblical Simplicity

The Hebrews left most of their possessions behind when they fled Egyptian slavery, and most of Israel's prophets warned against a societal emphasis on material possessions.

"Woe to them that are at ease," cries Amos, "that lie upon beds of ivory, and stretch themselves upon their couches, and eat the lambs out of the flock,...that drink wine in bowls, and anoint themselves with the chief ointments," neglecting devotion to God and service to the poor (6:1, 4, 6). "But let judgment run down as waters, and righteousness as a mighty stream" (5:24).

Jesus consistently emphasized simplicity in living, which He practiced throughout His private years in Nazareth and during His public ministry, and He demands simplicity of us:

> Therefore I say unto you, Take no thought for your life, what
> ye shall eat, or what ye shall drink; nor yet for your body,
> what ye shall put on. Is not the life more than meat, and the
> body than raiment?... But seek ye first the kingdom of God,
> and his righteousness; and all these things shall be added unto
> you. (Matthew 6:25, 33)

"The central point of the Discipline of Simplicity is to seek the kingdom of God and the righteousness of his kingdom *first* and then everything necessary will follow in its proper order," writes Richard J. Foster in *Celebration of Discipline*. "Everything hinges upon maintaining the 'first' things first." Nothing must come before God. The love of God is the first and the greatest of all commandments.[1]

The biblical mandate is clear and emphatic. Jesus exhorts us, urging material simplicity, at the very center of our lives: "Lay not up for yourselves treasures upon earth, where moth and rust doth corrupt, and where thieves break through and steal: but lay up for yourselves treasures in heaven, where neither moth nor rust doth corrupt, and where thieves do not break through nor steal: for where your treasure is, there will your heart be also" (Matthew 6:19–21).

This, of course, is a choice. Dallas Willard writes and has preached: "The vision of life in the kingdom through reliance upon Jesus makes it possible for us to *intend* to live in the kingdom as he did. We can actually *decide to do it.*... That means first of all to trust him, rely on him, to count on him.... If we do not count on him as the One, we will have no adequate vision of the kingdom."[2]

What does this mean for us who live in cities, with thousands of commercial opportunities available to us to see, to smell, to hear, to touch?

Downtown, you don't see the lilies of the field to which Jesus refers, so you may not consider them. This message may sound countercultural in the extreme. And yet, throughout the ages, people have managed to live it without becoming ascetics or monastics.

Testimony of Simplicity

A. W. Tozer is a good example. Tozer, a devoted Methodist pastor, came to Southside Alliance Church in Chicago in 1928. He was in ministry thirty-one years. Thousands of listeners tuned in to his radio program *Talks from a Pastor's Study.* Amid a big city's turbulence, Tozer maintained an extraordinary depth of prayer and peace—and simplicity.

"One of the greatest hindrances to internal peace which the Christian encounters is the common habit of dividing our lives into two areas—the sacred and the secular," he explained.

A simpler way of life—one not so divided—was his solution. Tozer suggested that Jesus Christ is "our perfect example and he [Jesus] knew no divided life. 'I do always those things that please him,' was his brief summary of his own life as it related to the Father (John 8:29)." This was the unifier and simplifier of Christ's life, and Tozer believed that we can similarly model our own lives—and as more than pious idealism. "It opens before us the possibility of making every act of our lives contribute to the glory of God."[3]

One of Tozer's most memorable prayers is one for inner simplicity:

Lord, make me childlike. Deliver me from the urge to compete with another for place or prestige or position. I would be simple and artless as a little child. Deliver me from pose and pretense. Forgive me for thinking of myself. Help me to forget myself and find my true peace in beholding Thee. That Thou may answer this prayer, I humble myself before Thee. Lay upon me Thy easy yoke of self-forgetfulness that through it I may find rest. Amen.[4]

A century earlier, a successful businessman lived out the sentiments of this prayer. Thomas Garrett of Wilmington, Delaware, held his goods lightly. His simple life was wholly dedicated to God and others as he kept a station or safe house on the Underground Railroad. The renowned African American conductor Harriet Tubman was a friend of Garrett and led many escaping slaves to refuge in his home.

Within that home, Garrett hid hundreds of runaway slaves, an act that he felt called by God to do, risking all for the cause of freedom. Indeed, Garrett gave his all, repeatedly, and he was fined heavily for his choices. But his community, seeing his virtue, bought everything up at auction and put him back in business, including the business of freeing slaves, once again.[5]

How might we practice material simplicity—so that we might have more room and time for God, to that degree of heroic risk?

Letting Go

Francis of Assisi, son of a wealthy medieval businessman, famously renounced the worldly life for which he was intended, right in the center of the town square. After an experience at war, the young Francis decided he didn't want to follow his father as a prosperous cloth merchant. In a public, city setting, Francis removed his outer garments, threw them down before his shocked father, and renounced material wealth forever. This saint, one of the most beloved of all time, consistently embraced simplicity in all aspects of his spiritual, dedicated life.

He left an enduring legacy in the foundation of his Third Order: followers of the Franciscan rule who were laypeople, living in the world, sometimes in urban areas, drew many different kinds of people who sought greater devotion to God, while practicing the Franciscan way of radical simplicity.

Today, there are many other examples. Billy Graham, the famous evangelist, lives in a log cabin in North Carolina. John Michael Talbot, a successful musician and recording artist, chose to live simply with an ecumenical Christian community he founded in the Ozarks.

But can "ordinary" people like us practice daily simplicity?

In *Falling for God,* author Gary W. Moon recounts the story "about the man who loses his footing while inspecting the gaping beauty of the Grand Canyon. The ground begins to erode under his feet and he slides over the edge of a steep cliff. Grabbing wildly for life, he latches on to a scraggly bush growing from the side of the canyon wall. With his feet dangling in midair and his fingers entwined with thin, leafy limbs, he cries out, 'God, please help me!' Immediately a voice deeper than James Earl Jones's resonates from below. 'I'm here for you, son. Let go. I've got you.' A few seconds pass in silence as beads of sweat begin to emerge on the man's forehead. Then he cries out again, 'Anyone got a better idea?'"[6]

Sometimes, surrender and simplification seem just that terrifying. It's difficult to change, hard to let go of familiar ways. It takes God's grace to go beyond the fear.

How do we get such grace?

We can begin by asking for it. I try to remind myself that I can take small steps and that simplicity is empty as an exercise in and of itself. Simplicity means nothing if I lose sight of God's love.

The challenge for me is this: I live in an expensive city. I've come to terms with the fact that I'll never be able to "live large" here. I'm no longer a surgeon's daughter. I can't afford many of the luxuries and pleasures available to the rich. When I was growing up, I was given costly clothes, a panoply of restaurant dining, house seats at Broadway shows. And yet, my family was not a happy one. When I think about that, I can come to accept my adult reality. I can still enjoy the city, but in moderation, with greater simplicity. I've found peace, not bitterness, in accepting this way of life. There's a certain freedom that comes with it, and more space for God.

That is exactly the point, David Yount writes in *Spiritual Simplicity:* "The great Beethoven interpreter, Alfred Brendel, suggests that the difference between a great pianist and a merely competent one, is that the true artist knows how to measure the silences between notes. You may believe that you are pressing the right buttons and striking the correct keys in your life, yet the result may be a busy cacophony."[7] Inner simplicity leaves more room for those necessary spaces between too many notes.

This doesn't mean that spiritual people in the city are called to become ascetics. In fact, Scripture doesn't condone asceticism taken to the extreme. "Scripture declares consistently and forcefully that the creation is good and to be enjoyed," Richard Foster says so beautifully. "Asceticism makes an unbiblical division between the good spiritual world and an evil material world." The Judeo-Christian tradition emphasizes the glory of what God has made.[8]

Inner Simplicity

The busy city of Boston taught me a great deal about simplicity. I learned from another beloved mentor, my first editor, who helped me develop my first novel. There was a great age difference between Anne Barrett and me—nearly fifty years. I was at the start of my career; she was nearing the end of hers. Nevertheless, there was a special chemistry between us and a deep friendship, a closeness that transcends our separation by her death.

Anne lived alone in a pleasant, and simple, apartment. She enjoyed beauty and had shelves filled with weathered, well-bound books. Her furniture was comfortable and a bit worn. Her fireplace was the focal point of her living room, and over it hung a treasured painting: a still life of a simple bowl of apples.

I remember sitting in front of the hearth with Anne, looking at the painting and talking of many things.

It's only when I look back that I see Anne's life as a model of simplicity, the kind that didn't advertise itself but made room for her own spirituality, of which we often spoke. Anne wasn't interested in status, style, or deal making. She had seen past those things and developed an emphasis on friendship and, increasingly, privately, on spirituality. As we worked together just before her retirement on developing my second novel, we spoke more often of the spiritual dimension.

The new novel was about another Anne—Anne Hutchinson, an early religious leader in Boston. I remember those graced afternoons of talk before the fire and the simple suppers I shared with the modern Anne. In her life, as Foster writes, "simplicity set[s] possessions in proper perspective."[9] Anne's modeling of this, quite unconsciously, was as valuable to me, a young writer, as was her invaluable editorial guidance.

Anne Barrett introduced me to a spiritual figure she much admired and whose memory has remained with me: Dag Hammarskjold, secretary-general of the United Nations for eight years, who was killed in a plane crash in 1961. After his death, the depth of his private faith became known. A manuscript titled *Markings* was found in his apartment, with authorization to publish it. My mentor and I shared this volume as we sat by her hearth and talked of the integration of the material and the spiritual.

Like Anne, Hammarskjold had come from a privileged background and had also found a need for a spiritual dimension. He had struggled with the balance of his commitment to God and the relationship between faith and duty; his personal faith had much to do with his very public position—and his peacemaking positions. Although this famous man was powerful and sophisticated, living a lifestyle that was not ascetic, there was a certain focused simplicity about his thought. When he was elected to the position of secretary-general in 1953, his notation in his journal was "Not I, but God in me."[10]

Inner simplicity is what Hammarskjold cultivated. In the midst of an exceptionally busy life in many of the world's busiest cities (and often, a glamorous one), he made room for God and for reflection. "The best and most wonderful thing that can happen to you in this life is that you should be silent and let God work and speak," he wrote.[11]

Hammarskjold experienced that when you make way for inner simplicity, you make way for the spiritual life. "I don't know Who, or what, put the question," he wrote. "I don't even remember answering. But at some moment I did answer *Yes* to Someone—or Something—and from that hour I was certain that existence is meaningful and that, therefore, my life, in self-surrender, had a goal.... After that, the word 'courage' lost its meaning, since nothing could be taken from me."[12]

Voluntary Simplicity

Oh, to feel that "Yes" of the urbane Hammarskjold. Imagine how it could usher in a way to live more simply in a distracting cityscape.

Voluntary simplicity is a way to deal with this dilemma. "Living simply is not about rejecting the material comforts of life," Linda Breen Pierce writes in her book, *Choosing Simplicity.* "However, it does involve unburdening our lives, living more lightly and with fewer distractions."[13]

In a city, where there are so many distractions, it may be more difficult to live more lightly. City dwellers are surrounded by seductive shop windows and commercial displays, as I noticed from the time I was a child. But there's a way to enjoy the creativity of these windows and their imaginative designs without having to purchase everything we see.

Spiritual simplicity is not the same as bitter deprivation. A woman I know is soon to be evicted from the room she rents. She still finds joy in the things of the senses but finds that her situation is bringing her into a closer relationship with God. Although this is a stressful time for her, it is a graced time as well. She appreciates life's simple pleasures as never before and as gifts from God's loving hand.

Simplicity takes different forms for each of us. You may decide, for example, that you need fewer clothes, fewer items of jewelry or gadgets. I may see that I need a smaller, less luxurious apartment, less expensive vacations. But as Richard Foster points out so wisely, sacrifices for simplicity mean less if we don't redirect our attention to what really matters. For those with a desire for more spiritual lifestyles, such sacrifice frees up more time and energy for God: "To receive what we have as a gift from God is the first inner attitude of simplicity. We live by grace even when it comes to 'daily bread.' We are dependent upon God for the simplest elements of life: air, water, sun.... When we are tempted to think that what we own is the result of our personal efforts, it takes only a little drought or a small accident to show us once again how utterly dependent we are."[14]

Is Simplicity Grim?

Is spiritual simplicity something only for Puritans? Is it a call to the joyless, the drab, and the rigidly virtuous?

I believe that's a popular misconception and an inaccurate one as well. When I wrote about a Puritan lay leader, Anne Hutchinson, I found her life to be an integration of simplicity and abundance. In Boston, she lived in a large and commodius house that she generously opened to the community for prayer meetings.

As Hutchinson might have noted, the Bible doesn't call us to be sour or dour. The Levitical codes don't prohibit joy. Jesus, in Matthew 25, assures us that God knows and understands our needs. And in His parable about the man who discovers the treasure in the field, Jesus tells us that the man acted with joy when he sold all he had to buy that field (see Matthew 13:44). There is joy too at the wedding at Cana, where Jesus turns water into wine (see John 2:1–10), and heaven is imaged as a banquet or a marriage feast.

In fact, simplicity may free us from certain anxieties, so that we may experience more joy and different kinds of celebration. "The secret of simple enjoyment is paying attention and cultivating taste," Yount writes in *Spiritual Simplicity*. "I cannot see the sky if I am looking at my feet or worrying about my job.... I will never enjoy anything unless I pay it the courtesy of my attention and seek to widen my world."[15]

New Joy

Making time for God not only widens our world, it opens us to a new kind of joy. Recently, at a contemporary urban church, simple and unadorned, I witnessed an extraordinary liturgy. A choir from Tanzania sang with such joy, its music brought listeners to tears. As the choir half marched, half danced down the aisle singing, the entire congregation seemed swept up in a transcendent moment of pure praise, gratitude, and grace.

"Celebration transforms the ordinary and can even create something extraordinary. Atmospheric conditions following a storm occasionally favor the formation of a rainbow. Rainbows are always unexpected, and many people miss them altogether," writes David Yount.[16] We are over-scheduled, we rush from event to event, and we don't have time to experience the moment. "Simplicity is senseless unless it lays open spaces in our lives that can be filled with grace."[17]

Mindfulness, attention to God in the present moment, is one way. As urban people, we cannot often run to Walden Pond or a retreat house for relief from clutter, commercial demands, and sensory overload.

But we can simplify how much we do, how much we consume, how much we spend, how much we schedule, so that there's space and openness for God's grace. I know that when I'm open to that grace, I can sense God's presence in the lit streets of a busy, complex city.

Status and Simplicity

The struggle, of course, is this: simplicity and spirituality may not be where the rewards appear most alluring. You might even think it's impossible to follow the dictates of a city lifestyle and a life of spiritual simplicity.

Consider the power of boards of directors, where the elite come together—or the power breakfast that certain hotels are known to host. And what about power lunches at fashionable watering holes noted by the dining guides of midsize cities. The demographics may shift, but there's always a power lunch somewhere.

In a recent *Washington Post* article, the Palm Restaurant is cited as a power lunch venue, as it has been for more than three decades. Vernon Jordan, a regular at the Palm, is quoted: "It's seeing and being seen. It's a happening."

Tommy Jacomo has run this "happening" restaurant for thirty-four years. "Everyone looks around and whispers," he says. "This is where the elite meet to eat." When asked why regulars go to the Palm so often, political advisor James Carville says, "I don't know. I mean, why do I have twenty pairs of socks and wear the same two?"[18]

There is a certain excitement about being a part of the urban elite: a power player. But in Washington DC, for example, these positions tend to change with administrations. In other cities, CEOs may suddenly lose their perches, as we have seen in recent years at Enron and Hewlett-Packard, to name only two instances. The world is a chancy place, and power tends to shift.

What stands throughout the years is the simple joy in the words of Thomas Kelly's classic *A Testament of Devotion,* to which I often refer: "Eternity is at our hearts, pressing upon our time-torn lives, warming us with intimations of an astounding destiny, calling us home unto Itself. Yielding to these persuasions, gladly committing ourselves in body and soul, utterly and completely…is the beginning of true life. It is a dynamic center.… It…illuminates the face of God and casts new shadows and new glories upon the faces of men." And perhaps most telling, is the next, cautionary, line: "It is a seed stirring to life if we do not choke it."[19]

We can choke it, if we choose, without a certain amount of simplicity and without a certain degree of attentiveness, it seems, to the "spaces between the notes."

Urban people, who are so quick, so smart about getting places, are well equipped to find more of those spaces where grace can flood in: grace that lasts.

—oooo—

Blessed be the LORD, because he hath heard the voice of my
    supplications.
The LORD is my strength and my shield; my heart trusted in him,
    and I am helped: therefore my heart greatly rejoiceth; and
    with my song will I praise him. (Psalm 28:6–7)

CURES FOR *Soulsickness* IN THE CITY

Stop: Read and Receive

1. Are you drawn to the sparkling and sophisticated wares in big-city stores? Can you enjoy an object's beauty, craftsmanship, and color without necessarily owning what you see?

2. When you reflect honestly on your needs, do you find yourself dominated by shopping and consumption? Do you shop when you want to feel better about yourself or your life—and do you do this instead of turning to life's spiritual side?

3. Most of us are dependent to some degree on the latest technological offerings. Ask yourself: Has my dependence gone so far that I've no sense of passion for or dependence on God?

4. In what ways (name three) do you need more, more, more of material things and less, less, less of life's spiritual dimension?

Yield: Reflect, Journal, or Discuss

5. Does your faith seem more like a fairy tale than the realities of work, achievement, salary, and status? Do you pursue these at the cost of relationships with other people and with God?

6. How can you simplify your life? Have you accumulated too much stuff, too many things that you don't really use? What can you do with this excess baggage? How can you share what you have with those who have not?

7. Make a written plan to inventory your life. Begin with areas of activity or your roles (for example, as a worker, spouse, parent) or even rooms of your home. Identify what

clutters your spaces and time. Now ask what comes between you and God in each area.

8. Jesus urges us to be mindful of the poor, and the Hebrew prophets warn us against extravagance. How can you bring your life into a closer alignment with this call?

Go: Experience and Engage

9. Read the gospel story of the rich young ruler who turned away from Jesus (see Matthew 19:16–24). List the possession with which you may identify too strongly.

10. Journal about some of your simple joys that are *not* material.

11. Note the simple gifts that you can give to others: time (when? for what?), a poem, baked brownies, prayers (continue the list). Act on one such way of giving this week.

12. Make a "Thank You List" to God at the end of each week this month. Review at the end of the month. Keep the list going, and note how this makes you feel and what you discover about the blessings you've been given.

FINDING GOD IN CHAOS

The Gateway to Peace

I once asked a busy urban physician how he was.
"Overworked," he said. "How's your life?"
"Stressful," I admitted.

"Tell me about it." He grinned.

"Can you find spirituality in this city?" I asked.

"Why not?" he shot back.

"Well, there's no letup—"

"But," he interjected, "we have the *park.*"

"True."

"And"—he looked triumphant—"we have the *Met.*"

"How can I argue with that?"

"My prescription for you," said the doctor, "go to church. Then to the park. *And go to the Met.*" He paused. "Try the theater too."

I'll always remember the first time I saw a revival of Thornton Wilder's *Our Town.* For me, the play was not only a cultural event but a spiritual

experience. Although set in a small New England town, the story spoke to
the city dweller in me. In the third act, the heroine, Emily, has died; her
spirit is acclimating to its new condition. The play's narrator comments that
we all know there is something eternal in us. "All the greatest people who
ever lived have been telling us that for five thousand years, and yet you'd be
surprised how people are always losing hold of it."[1]

With the narrator, Emily's spirit goes back to her girlhood kitchen,
where she is deeply moved by the sacred amid the ordinary things of life.
How rarely do we recognize this, she realizes. "Oh, Mama," she says to
her busy mother, "just look at me one minute as though you really saw
me… *Let's look at one another.*"[2]

How often this is true for us in cities: we don't take that time to see
one another, and to see the eternal, the presence of God, in others.

I remember coming out of that theater and looking at everything on
the street in a new light, in the light of God's eternity. But as *Our Town's*
narrator predicted, I've too often lost hold of that sense of really seeing,
that feeling of being present with all around me and in front of me. Yes,
that vision, that sense comes back, but for me it takes deliberation, intention, often through meditation upon God's will and ways, in reflecting
upon the arts—arts in the city centers that present them.

Holy Halls

Opera houses, symphony halls, and theaters are great artistic centers, in
both large and small metropolitan areas. Almost every town has a performance hall or museum or gallery that houses such beauty, whether
performance or painting or sculpture; these are sacred spaces where the
arts themselves are eternal mediators of the Holy.

In our own time, Stephen Sondheim, speaking at Carnegie Hall,
called that amazing place a kind of cathedral. In all eras, the arts have
been linked with sacred space. Think of Michelangelo's dazzling frescoes
on the ceiling of the Sistine Chapel, his world-famous *Pietà* in St. Peter's
Basilica, his equally famous statue of David in Florence. Think of Bach,
Mozart, and Mendelssohn, all of whom were steeped in liturgical music

and thrived in cities. These are only a few examples of the urban linkage between spirituality and the arts.

It's always been so. The ancient Greeks saw their theaters as semi-liturgical centers where drama was meant to have a moral and spiritual function: to strike the soul with "pity and awe" (*awe* is sometimes translated as "terror"). This is the same effect that Shakespeare's great tragedies have had on audiences through the centuries.

After the Dark Ages, theater reemerged from the worship of the church itself, where High Mass was as dramatic as it was holy. The Easter story was reenacted as it was read during the liturgy: the gospel account of the three women who discovered the empty tomb of Jesus and learned of the Resurrection. This reenactment was gradually expanded, then extended to encompass other Bible stories.

Throughout the Middle Ages, these brief plays came to be presented on a series of traveling pageant wagons. The dramas shown there were designed to lift the spirits of the audience to the Holy and to bring alive the accounts of people and events in the Bible. In different ways since that time, people have been deeply moved by theatrical productions, which have always had their greatest concentration in cities, from London's theater district—the West End—to Manhattan's Broadway and your town's civic theater.

Art and Spirituality

"The creative arts engage the whole being—body, mind, and spirit," according to a report from the Psychotherapy and Spirituality Institute. "Many spiritual and religious traditions have relied on the arts as a source of healing and as a pathway to accessing and sharing spirituality and the experience of God. Creative human expression and the shared appreciation of creative arts…serve as a bridge between these realms."[3]

The realms of the arts and spirituality dovetail beautifully in city centers for the performing arts. This is true for me, even when there's no performance, as these centers often have soaring architecture that uplifts the spirit and reminds me of a cathedral's space. Think of the art exhibits and pluming fountains at the cultural centers in your town. Inside, there is a hush in those great halls that seems resonant with many performances past and imagined that awaken the spirit to reach beyond the self.

In Washington DC, there are people who gravitate to the Kennedy Center for the Performing Arts not only for performances of plays, ballet, opera, and music but for the quiet afternoons, when the Grand Foyer is still majestic, and its chandeliers glow and its plush carpets mute sound. Visitors, gazing upward, are stilled and reverent in this space, where I've never heard a raised voice. This structure is a good place for quiet contemplation in the middle of this nation's busy capital city.

Urban Islands

From Boston to Chicago to Dallas to Los Angeles, such great centers exist as urban oases where the performing arts can still our chatter for a while, foster wonder, and feed our spiritual sensibilities, to help us make space in our busy lives for God.

Some of these centers are the very houses of worship where music and praise is constant, a more obvious confluence of the arts and spirituality. At holiday times especially, metropolitan churches offer a profusion of concerts, usually highlighting beloved sacred and seasonal music. But music is not reserved for the holidays alone.

In my neighborhood, within a few blocks of one another, there are weekly jazz vespers at a Lutheran church, organ recitals at a venerable synagogue and a Presbyterian church, and choral Evensong presented by the men and boys choir of a historic Episcopal church. Such spiritual oases are present in a multitude of cities and towns around the world.

I've noticed it's not just believers who flock to these presentations of sacred music in sacred spaces. Often the listeners are people from the community, not necessarily members of a given congregation, willing to even pay concert fees to hear uplifting compositions.

I heard one such man comment recently, "This music makes me believe in God all over again."

A longtime friend of mine, admittedly not a churchgoer, explains that for her, listening to music in a concert hall is "like going to church," an experience akin to prayerful contemplation.

Another city dweller who does go to church also finds a worshipful experience at her town's concert halls. Music, she observed, is the universal language that unites us all and opens our souls to the voice of the Holy Spirit.

Spiritual Peaks

Recently I attended a program at a large urban concert hall. A Beethoven concerto spilled over thousands of people whose faces were rapt, reverent, and sometimes tear stained. The concert made me feel prayerful and connected to everyone in that place as the music poured out, enveloping us.

"God is the uniquely Continuous Outpourer," writes Harold Best, author of *Unceasing Worship: Biblical Perspectives on Worship and the Arts.* "He cannot but give Himself, reveal Himself, pour Himself out…. This is the originating outpouring for which these mere words fail."[4]

I'm struck by how music is so often a way to worship God without words, and music itself becomes a spiritual oasis in a city where, if we listen rightly, all urban sounds combine in a unique symphony of their own.

Perhaps we've always understood the relationship between music and a state of worship. I'm reminded that angels are often depicted with harps and lutes and trumpets in their hands. King David also wrote an astonishing number of psalms that are sung and chanted to this day. One psalm in particular is addressed to the chief musician and exhorts all God's people to "make a joyful noise unto God, all ye lands: sing forth the honour of his name: make his praise glorious" (Psalm 66:1–2).

In Luke's gospel, the birth of Jesus was announced to attentive shepherds by "a multitude of the heavenly host praising God, and saying, Glory to God in the highest, and on earth peace, good will toward men"

(Luke 2:13–14). These words have become part of age-old traditional Christmas hymns, and hymnody itself has become an art. Clearly, God's praise and musical expression can draw us into a deeper spirituality.

Museums and Oases

As a child, I had two recurring wishes. One was to get locked inside a cathedral overnight, and the second was to get locked inside a museum. These were places of wonder and holiness for me, special echoing buildings with soaring inner space and a sacred hush about them. The light was different inside each place. The air seemed different too. Time seemed to stand still in both the church and the art hall; the veil between the material and spiritual worlds seemed to thin and grow transparent.

I've spent a lot of time in a museum's medieval wing, which almost seems like a church with many chapels. On some deep inner level, I always feel this way about any museum wing that displays religious art, and so many of these museums are visual oases in big cities. Such areas are worshipful places to me and to many others, who stand and gaze in awe at triptychs and paintings that strain to capture the wonder of heaven and earth, the Holy, in imagery.

As I look around at the others who share these spaces, I often see reverent and moved expressions on a diverse range of faces. The expression is the same on all these faces all around the world, as if seeing a mystery, a sacred secret, together. The images we find linger in our minds, and we seek their reminders. I noted one of many: in a busy downtown church office, a pastor has a beautiful screen saver, Fra Angelico's rendering of *The Annunciation* from the great city of Florence, Italy.

If I want to escape the busy streets of a big city for a few moments, my first impulse is to dodge into a church. My second impulse is to duck into an art museum, any art museum. Collections of religious art are not the only ones that inspire contemplation, of course. For me, most museums hold thousands of windows on the Holy through the paintings that hang on the walls.

A fruitful spiritual exercise is this: center or focus on an abstract painting and see God in the confluence of line and color. The shapes and structures of such artists as Mondrian and Ryder inevitably remind me of stained glass. The beauty of impressionist paintings—from Cezanne's apples to Monet's lily ponds—turn my mind and heart to the glory of God's creation. Other painters lead me to reflect upon the human condition; in a museum's stillness, I can find oases of contemplative quiet.

Paintings to Planets

Several years ago, an exhibition of Eastern Orthodox icons came to the Walters Gallery in Baltimore, Maryland. Long lines appeared around this museum as people waited patiently to enter the dim, hushed exhibit from which the icons shone forth with their compelling, otherworldly gazes and their halos of gold leaf.

Other kinds of museums can present spiritual oases, as well. For example, museums of natural history show us the wonder and glory of God's creation as a fossil or a fish bone becomes an object of contemplative prayer. In the words of Psalm 8, "O LORD our Lord, how excellent is thy name in all the earth! who hast set thy glory above the heavens" (verse 1).

Years ago at the famous National Air and Space Museum in Washington DC, a series of concerts was given in the planetarium. The lights were dimmed, the "heavens" were illuminated, and chamber music surrounded the crowd present, which included me. It was one of the most memorable spiritual oases I've ever experienced. We were bathed in silvery light, listening to oboes and strings. The faces around me were rapt, uplifted, and reverent.

A phrase from Psalms expresses this time even better: "When I consider thy heavens, the work of thy fingers, the moon and the stars, which thou hast ordained"(8:3).

Thinking on this, experiencing the beauty of the heavens, I'm speechless.

Art and Contemplation

Sister Wendy Beckett, a cloistered nun for most of her life, has become a renowned art commentator and critic for public television. Her series on all eras of Western art has been immensely popular, insightful, and informative. Now a hermit on the grounds of a monastery, Sister Wendy teaches a special approach to art museums—how time in the art museum can make one a more spiritually sensitive person.

"Art," she told interviewer Bill Moyers, "has given me enormous joy and has increased my capacity to accept darkness and pain. All art that really draws us to look deeply at it is spiritual. Sacred art is 'spiritual' at its most profound and emphatic."

How interesting that she doesn't think that religious art is necessarily always spiritual. But "art helps us to be perpetually 'there'—in the moment." This kind of presence is so important because "God is coming to us every moment but we are not noticing that he is coming. Art helps us to be a more attentive person."

She props up a relic of a painting on a small stand in her hermitage and looks at the work, just looks and waits for the work to speak to her. This way of looking and waiting is done with patience and without defensiveness. Instead, Sister Wendy says she does this as a way to "surrender" herself to the work before her. By "surrendering," she means that "you are not going to defend yourself from the ramparts of your own ego—you are going to open yourself to what is given."

This reference to self-surrender is the language of prayer: the language that's congruent with practicing the presence of God.

"Art," she says, "will take you into uncharted realms. It lifts us out of the confines of our ego, out of the traps many people are in: relationships, mortgages, worries.... Art takes you into something bigger than yourself, untouched by our littleness and anxieties."

This is a great spiritual oasis, and, Sister Wendy believes, everyone has the potential to enter it—to see art in the spiritual way she does. This is a hopeful and inspiring thought for harried city dwellers: we can enter a museum and find ourselves in a quiet, powerful encounter with God.[5]

Kathleen Norris, a Presbyterian who explored her evangelical faith at a Benedictine monastery, would agree. She found a special moment on the busy streets in downtown Chicago, where she recalled the Art Institute, Symphony Hall, and the old Opera House in her book *The Cloister Walk*. Especially vivid was a childhood Christmas when her father took her and her brother to the Loop: "It was a bitterly cold day, and when we passed by a Salvation Army band, my father, who was wearing his Navy great-coat, stopped and offered to relieve the trumpeter for a few songs. A Methodist pastor's son, he knew all the hymns.... The bell ringer asked if I'd like to ring the bells, which I did with great enthusiasm, beaming up at everyone who put in coins."[6]

Prayerful Parks

In today's cityscapes, it's easy to forget that we human beings did not make our world. All around us we see the wonders and fruits of architecture, building, and engineering—the great sweep of avenues, the intricate threading of streets, the spans of bridges, and soaring skyscrapers like Chicago's famous Sears Tower.

All city planners, however, have known that the human spirit also needs to be in touch with nature, and these planners have acted accordingly. Some of the world's most beautiful parks and natural spiritual oases exist in the midst of bustling cities: Kew Gardens in London, the Tuileries Garden in Paris, Manhattan's Central Park, Chicago's Grant Park, Denver's Cheeseman and City Parks, the Boston Common—the list is rich and long.

Parks have always been magnets for the city population and offered places for quiet reflection: sweeping lawns, swaying trees, rock formations, benches. As a child, I remember the holy hush of a great park after a snowfall; the trees bent together in places that seemed like secret chapels. The sacredness of God's creation touches us in such places and prompts our contemplation. The great American poet Emily Dickinson observed:

> To make a prairie it takes a clover and one bee,—
> One clover, and a bee,

And revery.
The revery alone will do
If bees are few.[7]

Dickinson, a New England Protestant, didn't leave her home and garden for most of her fifty-six years (1830–86). In nature, the poet found a great resource for her art and her theology—a deep well of spiritual nourishment that never ran dry for her. She expresses her spirituality often and so beautifully:

I never saw a moor,
I never saw the sea;
Yet know I how the heather looks
And what a wave must be.

I never spoke with God,
Nor visited in heaven;
Yet certain am I of the spot
As if the chart were given.[8]

Rocking the Heart

As a child, I had a sense of God's nearness the first time I climbed into a rowboat on a pond in a park. I remember the smell of moss and sun-baked wood, and what seemed to be a vast expanse of sparkling green water. And I felt a presence greater than the park, the city, myself. I was almost too awed to get into that boat. The pond seemed to be alive.

Finally I decided it was God who had spread it out and would keep the boat safe. My father, who rowed, often recalled how I came to love this excursion and refused, for several minutes, to get out of the boat again. I couldn't articulate this at the time, but that pond had become a sacred space for me, and it still is.

And that's because "each place matters, each place is alive," Robert

M. Hamma suggests in his book *Landscapes of the Soul.*[9] You can sense the presence of the Divine everywhere, he says, if you're attentive.

I thought of this recently on a stroll through the park. Many people were sitting on park benches, looking deeply attentive: to the zigzag of squirrels on the path before them, to the movement of wind through the trees, to the sound of water splashing in a nearby fountain.

As mentioned earlier, fountains are also places of spiritual refreshment in cities. Located in Central Park near a heavily trafficked crosstown street, there rises the tranquil *Angel of the Waters* at Bethesda Fountain. The fountain's inspiration is a verse from the gospel of John that describes a pool at Bethesda, where an angel, stirring the waters, cured pilgrims who came to be healed. The meaning of the word *Bethesda* is "place of mercy," and this place, with its lovely bronze angel, is one of many places for centering and focusing prayer and contemplation. I've gone there feeling hot and frazzled, but when I stay and listen to the water's music, a sense of peace comes over me and follows me home.

A tear-shaped area, over two acres large, is set aside as Strawberry Fields in honor of John Lennon, who was murdered nearby. The area is landscaped with plants from all over the world and marked by a Neapolitan plaque that reads, "Imagine," the title of the famous Lennon song. Strawberry Fields is a meditative spot, while the larger spaces of this park have been venues for religious services: Billy Graham's evangelistic crusade in 1991 drew crowds that packed the place, Pope John Paul II celebrated a mass on the Great Lawn in 1995, and the Dalai Lama spoke four years later in the East Meadow.

We've seen the beauty of the Reflecting Pool in Washington DC, and many of us have been deeply moved by the extraordinary Vietnam War Memorial, also in the parks of our nation's capital. If we're quietly attentive to any favorite spot in a park and if we view it with the contemplative awareness of Sister Wendy, we can easily be touched by God's presence in another spiritual oasis.

Thomas Merton, writing in Kentucky, beautifully expresses the way we can feel in such places: "Today, Father, this blue sky lauds you. The delicate green and orange flowers of the tulip poplar tree praise you. The distant blue hills praise you, together with the sweet-smelling air that is full of brilliant light.… I too, Father, praise you, with all these my brothers, and they give voice to my own heart and to my own silence."[10]

Houses of Prayer

Cities are rich in diverse houses of worship too. "Some form of spirituality is essential to human life," begins *The Spiritual Traveler* by Edward F. Bergman. "And city dwellers follow many paths of find spiritual peace and strength." Houses of worship count among a city's "most splendid monuments," Bergman notes—vibrant communities as well—and many still leave their doors open for the visitor in search of a more overly religious oasis.[11]

Bergman's book helps you acclimate to various religions' houses of worship, a practice that can deepen your personal spirituality by visiting houses of worship that are not your own. You may not choose to worship at the places you visit, but you can't ignore the reverential hush in all such places. A city's diversity of churches, synagogues, temples, and meetinghouses, helps you develop your sense of tolerance—and your sense of sacred space and holy ground.

As a small child, I was taken to St. Patrick's Cathedral, where I felt something inexplicable: amid the scents of incense and wax, flowers and floor polish, there was a palpable sense of prayer. In those days, I heard more often the click of rosary beads than there are now perhaps, but it wasn't only that *tick-tick-tick* of sound that told me I was home. It was the rapt faces: it was the serene profile of my devout aunt, through the white transparency of her mantilla.

Years later, I was taken by a beloved school teacher into Notre Dame, on the Isle de la Cité in Paris, and felt again that sense of sacred space, a place beyond words. In the middle of the crowded city of Paris, this medieval cathedral has held many in its hushed, holy nave. My teacher took us next to a cathedral outside of Paris, visible from the Eiffel Tower, fifty miles away in Chartres: once a thriving medieval town.

Chartres Cathedral is a legendary spiritual oasis which has drawn me back again and again—once to write about it in *Hemispheres* magazine. "Above me, the cathedral rises on its hill like a great horned, magical creature caught in afternoon light." The nave itself is a lake of blue light, and the storied stained-glass windows glow like liquid lace. The windows tell the story of holy men and women—and also the townspeople who lived and worked in the shadow of the great cathedral.

"These were people who paused at noon when the tower's bells rang the Angelus—people whose entire lives were lived in the presence of sacred space."[12] And we seek it still.

Thousands of pilgrims visit this cathedral and many others every year, and visitors are consistently hushed and awed by these soaring edifices. We're inextricably linked to those who went before us: we reach beyond our small, singular lives for some quiet time in the Holy One's presence. This can happen in any house of worship, of course, not only a great medieval cathedral, if we're willing to pause, to be quiet, and to enter into these rich and varied metropolitan oases.

Home Base

Of course, a spiritual oasis doesn't always have to be out there in a park, church, museum, or concert hall. Many of us find a need to set aside a little space of our own, in our apartments, for prayer or meditation, for our more focused time with God.

Some people have a home office that can also hold an area set apart in some way for prayer. Others let a room do double duty. People who spend a lot of time in the kitchen may choose that as their sacred space. I've seen many a prayer on a kitchen wall, as well as picture variations of what's commonly known as *The Sacred Heart* (the heart of Christ encircled by a crown of thorns, often featured upon an artist's likeness of Christ) and Albrecht Durer's famous sketch (and also sculpture) of praying hands.

Many years ago, a busy urban housewife and cook said she prayed best with the smells of bread baking around her; she also found the act of washing dishes by hand a meditative experience. The sound of running water, a kettle coming to boil—these are cues for me, from childhood, to feel safe and prayerful.

I used to have a small study that doubled as a prayer room and held a rocking chair, where one of my Carmelite friends, on an extern assignment, said her afternoon prayers on a graced afternoon. This dormer room had unfinished walls around the desk, where I could hang pictures that were spiritually evocative for me.

Now I have the corner of a room where I can set out what makes this space sacred: a candle, an icon, a flower, a stone from the holy island of Iona, and a Bible. My bedside table has other spiritual reading material and other devotional objects of spiritual meaning for me.

Everyone has a different way of setting out individual sacred space. There are no magic formulas for these, and the spaces may change according to the season, the liturgical segment of the year, and of course the faith tradition that anchors us.

A friend of mine defines her corner area with a white light and a white Bible, from which she reads sections of the book of Proverbs before a hectic day as an administrator at an urban university. In another room, in December, she sets out the menorah that she and her husband treasure. Another friend has a prayer room, like a chapel, with a cross and tokens from spiritual venues all over the world.

Long ago, I was in a prayer group with a fellow believer who only wanted a plain, well-lit space where he would sit and "seek the Light."

You create the oasis that's right for your own spiritual practice; I like to think of all the different kinds of people, perhaps at twilight, saying evening prayers, such as vespers, or simple table graces. The dusk shifts and deepens. Traffic, like a great tide, swells and recedes and flows again. The pattern of apartment lights changes, some distant ones flickering like votive candles as the darkness folds down. And there, across the cities of the world, if we take the time to notice, we can feel ourselves united by a spiritual sense of homecoming.

There, in your home oasis, my Carmelite friends advise:

Take a few minutes to enter into the silence and hear God speaking His word of love in your heart. To learn the language of God,
you must take a few quiet moments to be still. Of course a million
things will crowd into your mind and heart—all the things that
scream for your attention—good things, things that need to be
done. But wait, just take a few moments to hear God speaking.
Let Him touch your heart with His love. Let Him calm your fears
and anxieties. Let Him show you the many ways He comes to you
every day. Every moment He is coming, every moment is full of
His caring presence, every moment He is helping you. Close your
eyes and let yourself be loved by the God of love and then spend
the rest of the day in dialogue with Him. No need to get on your
knees for this loving dialogue—talk to him as a friend.[13]

Inner Oases

Every week in houses of worship across the globe, prayers are offered for
peace in our cities. This, it is often said, begins within our own hearts.
As you pray for peace in your heart, you also ask God to form an oasis
there. You invite Him into your heart and mind; to be an instrument of
His peace, in the words of Saint Francis, you need to draw on that well
of peace inside. This isn't always easy, especially amid the activity of city
living. And yet, the cultivation of an inner oasis is not a new idea.

Around 1579, Saint Teresa of Avila wrote the great spiritual classic
The Interior Castle, one of the most famous Western books on contemplative prayer that has endured from century to century. The central image
of Saint Teresa's "inner oasis" is simple, though that doesn't mean that it's
shallow or facile; nor is her interior castle a frozen place where there's no
growth. The inner oasis Teresa writes about is all about growing spiritually
and progressing from mansion to mansion.[14]

"We have within us space for God, what I call 'Godspace'. This 'Godspace' is innate but we have been living our lives without it," writes Melvyn
Matthews in *Making Room for God: A Guide to Contemplative Prayer.* "We

do without it sometimes by conviction, but just as often by sheer neglect and the desire to fill our lives with something.... It is this sense of inner space, which is God-given, which is to be refound, and lovingly preserved within the human life and within the human soul."[15]

Each of us has inner "Godspace," and for each of us this space looks different.

Mine looks like the rowboat pond in a city park.

He that dwelleth in the secret place of the most High shall abide
    under the shadow of the Almighty.
I will say of the LORD, He is my refuge and my fortress: my God;
    in him will I trust.
Surely he shall deliver thee from the snare of the fowler, and from
    the noisome pestilence.
He shall cover thee with his feathers, and under his wings shalt
    thou trust: his truth shall be thy shield and buckler.
    (Psalm 91:1–4)

CURES FOR *Soulsickness* IN THE CITY

Stop: Read and Receive

1. Where do you find a spiritual oasis in the city? Does it help you connect with nature as in a park, or does it help you connect with the arts as in a museum or concert hall? Is your oasis in a house of worship or your own home?

2. How can you maintain a sense of spiritual oasis on a subway train or on a bridge, looking at a city's skyline, or walking around your neighborhood?

3. If you were to imagine yourself with God, where would you be? Write down on a postcard the images that come to mind, and carry it with you as a reminder.

4. Have you ever found a spiritual oasis in a relationship? in a sense of closeness and intimacy with another person? How have you found this relational oasis in prayer? in worship? in time spent practicing the presence of God?

Yield: Reflect, Journal, or Discuss

5. In the midst of a city, what moments from your past come to mind regarding a time or place when you felt very close to God? List such times and places so that they can be "imported" to your city as spiritual oases.

6. Does the presence of water give you that "oasis" feeling? Can you seek out a reservoir, lake, or river once a month or once a week and dedicate your time there to God?

7. Take a line from a daily Scripture reading and reflect on it through the day, bringing to mind the peace of reading as you do so.

Go: Experience and Engage

8. This month, set aside a time when you can visit an art museum or gallery to view a favorite painting as an act of contemplation and a time of prayer.

9. Make a lunch break into a spiritual oasis. Go to a house of worship once a week for a spiritual lunch—a time to feed your soul. Many downtown churches and synagogues have organ recitals or services at noontime. Decide if you can meet God by choosing a familiar house of worship or a different one to provide spiritual refreshment.

10. Spend an "oasis hour" with a friend in prayer.

11. Form a small prayer group that meets once a month for breakfast.

12. Sit quietly with a bowl of fruit or flowers and make their beauty an oasis on your dining table—a focal point for contemplation, wonder, and gratitude of and to the Holy One.

8

FINDING GOD IN GUTTERS
The Gateway to Giving

I t was January: freezing cold. And it was a day of evictions in Washington DC. The holidays were over, and people seriously behind in their rent could no longer be given leniency.

That afternoon, as I worked in my snug study, I received a call from someone in my parish. A weeping woman, I heard, was sitting in her easy chair on the street. The city was confiscating her furniture and forcing her from her apartment. Because I was a volunteer at a homeless shelter, I was asked what could be done.

I called around to various shelters that I knew and eventually found the woman a shelter with an empty bed; it was, as far as my sources knew, the last bed in any shelter for that night. I said a prayer that the right person would be sent to help this woman, and then I went back to my work: a piece of writing that had engaged my energies.

At dusk, I was called again. A minister had come to sit with the evicted woman, and the church had offered to store some of her things.

The storage had been done, but the minister had to leave—could I bring the woman some dinner?

I remember the rush of panic I felt as I heated food and packed it in a basket used previously to store magazines. In a fit of desperation, I threw in a pair of candlesticks, candles, and matches, and got in the car. At last, when I reached the woman whom I'll call Dana, I lost my preoccupation with myself, my failings, and my fears that I could not handle this situation.

Table for Two

Dana, an aging white woman in a thin coat, sat in her chair on the street, in front of one end of her dining table. The other end had been trucked away, along with the table's leaves. Stammering, I introduced myself and asked if she would like to go into the parish hall across the street—it would be warmer there. Dana looked up and shook her head. She couldn't bear to leave the remnants of her furniture, and she couldn't abandon her longtime home just yet.

And so, we had dinner together there on the street, while passersby stared and stepped around us. Dana was the one who made it a moving experience. She lit the candles and said a beautiful grace over the food. I listened to her talk about her life as the temperature dropped way below freezing. Even then, Dana resisted the idea of going to the shelter until finally, likening her situation to a shipwreck, she said she would get in the lifeboat—the warm bed that awaited her out there in the dark.

When I reflect on that evening, I realize that it was Dana who had turned a disaster into a blessing. She had also been my teacher and I, the reluctant helper. This woman, in the crisis of her life, showed me what real gratitude looked like, and I still see her face, illuminated by the candles, her eyes closed, and her smile as she thanked God for the supper.

This woman had shown me what real courage looked like as well. We left that easy chair, that favorite chair, *her* chair, on the street, but Dana did not look back in self-pity. She turned to God in trust and, eventually, was settled in a lifetime home for indigent women.

I didn't know, that January night, how her story would end. I only knew that God, through Dana, had given me an example of genuine grace under extraordinary pressure.

Tzedakah

All Western religious people can be proud of deep Jewish roots; I'm proud of mine. Jesus, a literate Palestinian Jew, would have known and spoken the word *tzedakah,* which is Hebrew for "acts of service." The word "goes beyond donating money" or sending a neighbor home with leftovers, Meredith Gould explains in her book *Deliberate Acts of Kindness.* "*Tzedakah* sees generosity as righteousness."[1] This is the righteousness that's an essential part of spiritual life, and the practice of tzedakah is what Jesus wanted all of us to grasp.

For traditional Jews, a special box is kept at home for the poor, and coins are routinely placed in the box. Eight levels of tzedakah may be demonstrated. At the first level, you give begrudgingly. At the next level, you give cheerfully but less than you should. The succeeding level is giving after being asked, and beyond that is giving without being asked. The second highest level of tzedakah is giving anonymously, and the highest level of all is "enabling the recipient to become self-reliant."[2]

Do you see how the concept of tzedakah challenges us to give to others, but asks us to reflect on our attitude toward giving itself?

In the nineteenth chapter of Leviticus, it's commanded that those who harvest grain leave a border of crops for gleaners, and those who keep vineyards must leave the fallen fruit for "the poor and stranger." The owner of a field or piece of productive property is seen as the steward of God's creation, and the steward must give to those in need a portion of what he has been given. It is notable too that room is left for the dignity of the needy ones, who can glean and gather on their own.

When we give, then, we are called to do service with respect for the one we serve. That's a challenge for each of us—to give without patronizing the recipient.

Charity in the City

The word *charity* comes from the Latin word *caritas,* for love. Throughout the gospels, Jesus challenges us to act out of love, even to our enemies. We are called, then, to give to others out of love, even for the stranger, even to those we view across various barriers. "Though I speak with the tongues of men and of angels, and have not charity, I am become as sounding brass, or a tinkling cymbal," Paul writes (1 Corinthians 13:1).

And why are we called to have charity and serve others? In Matthew 25:34–40, Jesus tells us a parable about a king who welcomes his subjects: "Come, ye blessed of my Father, inherit the kingdom prepared for you from the foundation of the world: for I was a hungred, and ye gave me meat: I was thirsty, and ye gave me drink: I was a stranger, and ye took me in: naked, and ye clothed me: I was sick, and ye visited me: I was in prison, and ye came unto me.… Inasmuch as ye have done it unto one of the least of these my brethren, ye have done it unto me."

In cities, the hungry, the thirsty, the ragged, and the broken are not cordoned off from those more fortunate. When you look around an urban locale, you see the full spectrum of human life. Prostitutes and drug addicts are part of the cityscape, along with the indigent. In the evenings, I see some of the city's poor gathering on church steps, where men and women construct personal shelters out of cardboard boxes. Sometimes I feel helpless as I watch, and I'm sure I'm not the only one. Many urban people watch the poor in our midst, and many find ways to serve them.

"How we treat the poor is how we treat God," Ronald Rolheiser states in his book *The Holy Longing.* "Reaching out, preferentially, to the poor is an essential component of the spiritual life. Your touch is Christ's touch."[3]

And who are the poor whom we are called to reach? The poor can be the materially impoverished, but there are other forms of poverty and need. There are the lonely, the lost, the sick, the imprisoned, the suffering, even the rude and the angry. They're waiting for us, even now.

"We serve God by serving others," Rick Warren says in *The Purpose-Driven Life: What on Earth Am I Here For?*[4] Because Jesus "measures greatness in terms of service, not status," Warren urges us to have "a servant heart." He notes that John Wesley was an admirable servant of God who conducted himself with the motto "Do all the good you can, by all the means you can, in all the ways you can, in all the places you can, at all the times you can, to all the people you can, as long as you ever can."

That might sound quite overwhelming at first, but in cities there are countless small steps to start living this way: Write a note to a shut-in. Be polite to the rude neighbor in the elevator. Listen, really listen, to a troubled friend. Drive a senior to a doctor's office. And in the city, there are so many ways to serve the poor, the hungry, the lonely, the ill, the impaired. Perhaps we all have a ministry if we are attentive to the possibility—and God's timing.

Susie Davis writes: "Even Old Testament prophets needed to be reminded of God's schedule. Isaiah found his life a wreck in the year that King Uzziah died. In a moment of despair...he searchingly looked to God for relief. God answered his questions with a question of His own. And peering into God's blueprint of his life, Isaiah took hold of his own readiness. 'And I heard the voice of the Lord, saying, *Whom shall I send* and *Who will go for us?* Then said I, *Here am I; Send me'* (Isaiah 6:8)."[5]

A prayer attributed to Teresa of Avila expresses this challenge, this call:

Christ has no body now but yours,
No hands but yours,
No feet but yours.
Yours are the eyes through which
Christ's compassion must look out on the world.
Yours are the feet with which
He is to go about doing good.
Yours are the hands with which
He is to bless us now.[6]

Prayerful reflection on these words reveals their power and their very personal challenge to each of us.

"As the cross is the sign of submission, so the towel is the sign of service," writes Richard J. Foster in *Celebration of Discipline.*[7] In the time of Jesus, it was customary to wash guests' feet before meals. This, however, was a task for servants and slaves—for those who were the least, on the social scale. But it was Jesus who took up the towel and filled a basin with water. He, the leader, the master, washed His followers' feet.

Jesus gave the fundamental model for servanthood and challenged His disciples to do as He had done. "If I then, your Lord and Master, have washed your feet; ye also ought to wash one another's feet. For I have given you an example, that ye should do as I have done to you" (John 13:14–15).

But what form should our service take?

Serving Through Prayer

In the midst of a city, our prayers form an offering of time and self if prayer is practiced with real feeling, not as a laundry list. Prayer is a way that urban people can serve the community at large. Whenever there's been a disaster, such as 9/11, Hurricane Katrina, or a bridge collapse in Minneapolis, the residents of cities have reached out to one another in prayer as well as in action. For them this isn't some kind of magical incantation; this is genuine, serious business, nor does this occur only in times of crises.

"If we truly love people," writes Richard J. Foster in his book *Prayer: Finding the Heart's True Home,* "we will desire for them far more than it is within our power to give them, and this will lead us to prayer. Intercession is a way of loving others. When we move from petition to intercession, we are shifting our center of gravity from our own needs to the needs and concerns of others. Intercessory prayer is selfless prayer, even self-giving prayer."[8]

Foster believes that in the "ongoing work of the kingdom of God, nothing is more important than intercessory prayer." He cites the intercessory prayers of Moses, on behalf of Joshua's fight for Jericho, as real, tangible service (see Exodus 17:8–13). Moses prayed so hard, with his arms lifted high, that Aaron and Hur were called in to help keep his arms braced upward. The prayers continued until the battle was won.[9]

Jesus asks us to practice prayer, especially intercessory prayer, even for those who are hostile, combative, or abusive to us. "Abide in me, and I in you," He said. "As the branch cannot bear fruit of itself, except it abide in the vine; no more can ye, except ye abide in me" (John 15:4).

Isn't it easy in the city to notice the fire truck racing to help, the near accident, the sidewalk altercation, and pass by without a thought of prayer? Isn't it like the priest and the Levite in the parable of the good Samaritan? But what happens when we can offer to help in action or in prayer, or both? How can we keep the face of a suffering stranger in our minds and hearts all day?

There is a wonderful story of a monk on Mount Athos, "the holy mountain" in Greece, home to many Greek Orthodox monasteries. In one, various monks managed different areas where laypeople came to work, but things didn't go so smoothly...except in one area alone. The monk who supervised this area was finally questioned by his brothers: how did he achieve such order, such ease in his workroom? The monk showed them a list that held his workers' names. Every evening, the monk said, he would go and pray earnestly, and sometimes with tears, for the people on his list: for their troubles, families, and needs. The people never knew of these prayers—all they knew was that, at work, things seemed to go well.[10]

The Homeless

Homeless people are a presence in all cities and are perhaps the most visible of the urban poor. We may have mixed reactions to them, however, and it is helpful to sort these feelings out before we engage in service to the homeless.

Sometimes, homeless people are seen as lazy, shirkers of work, or con artists. But, in fact, the largest percentage of homeless people are emotionally ill; many live on the streets after the "deinstitutionalization" of many patients in state psychiatric hospitals. There's also a sizable percentage of homeless people who are caught in cycles of addiction to alcohol or substances. Sometimes poor people are rendered homeless by a disaster: a devastating fire, the loss of health and employment, the death of a spouse. For the poor, once such a loss occurs, it's unusual for them to attain another home.

Many urban churches and synagogues offer meal programs for the homeless. There's a welcoming attitude at such programs, ranging from breakfast to dinner to the traditional soup kitchen. Volunteers can be involved with meal preparation or serving the food itself.

For several years I felt drawn to help prepare and serve lunch in shelters for homeless women. These shelters are well run and provide a wide array of other services to women who are in very real need. Rachael's Women's Center in Washington DC is only one of many urban shelters that offers hot lunches, laundry facilities, social workers' consultations, and safety, six days a week.

I have many memories of my time at the shelters. I recall one homeless woman contemplating a spray of dogwood on a battered table ("It reminds me of God," she said). Another woman painted a mural of inspirational figures on a dingy wall, and I remember feeling grateful to live in a city where I could witness such wonders.

There are also houses of worship that offer their space as sleeping quarters for homeless people. In one such shelter, mats are put down in a chapel, and there, homeless people are protected from crime as well from inclement weather. In many large cities, one sees the homeless gather at dusk in the doorways of churches, where bedrolls are laid out and cardboard boxes are used for some protection against the elements.

It's easier and safer for volunteers to offer help in the context of a feeding program or a well-run shelter. To find the right venue for you in your city, ask at your church or search on the Internet with the key words "soup kitchen." In many cities, a map will pop up and show locations where you can be of service.

Is Service Spiritual?

"It's service," someone once challenged me, "but is it spiritual?"

For the Hebrew prophets and for Jesus, there was no such dichotomy. Scripture teaches that we're all created in God's image, and however defaced that image has become, we're called to express our love for God and our love for others. The greatest commandments, Jesus said, are to love God and our neighbor.

It's not easy to develop an attitude of service, one free of a patronizing view or a certain curiosity or a self-congratulatory feeling. True service has a lot to do with attitude. It isn't helpful to be a Lady Bountiful–type or a put-upon martyr.

The first time I volunteered to help with supper in a shelter, I saw the side of service that can turn people off. It was a rainy night and the women were irritable. No one thanked us as we ladled out stew, and a fight broke out at one of the tables. There was a strong smell of wet wool and damp sneakers in the dining room, and I wondered if this kind of service was for me. I don't know if I felt endangered or out of my depth. And that is an important aspect of service—it's not an occasion to make oneself feel saintly.

Servanthood

There's a side of servanthood that calls us to let people minister to us. So often on Holy Thursday, I've seen people who would rather do the foot washing than have their own feet washed. In serving, as well as being served, we approach sensitive boundaries of personal space; we need to work with our own feelings of vulnerability and humility if we're to let someone else have the joy of giving to and blessing us.

At Rachael's Women's Center, I remember a homeless woman singing "Happy Birthday" to me, not because it was my birthday, but because she knew the song. The shelter director later told me that the woman, for the first time in a long time, had something to give.

If we're to express our spirituality among a city's poor, we have to come to terms with our own internal poverty, our own areas of neediness, and realize that the act of service doesn't make us magnanimous or superior. We're in it together.

It is so important for us all to feel we have something to give. A homeless woman used to come to coffee hour at my parish. She did partake of the coffee and pastries when those were offered. But in return, she gave each server an envelope of autumn leaves she had collected, carefully dated. I found such an envelope recently; the leaves had turned to dust, but her act of giving is fresh as an October morning in my mind.

Loving the "Unlovable"

Mother Teresa of Calcutta saw no dichotomy between prayer and service. She balanced her day with both. "Never think that a small action done to your neighbor is not worth much," she advises. "It's not how much we do that is pleasing to God, but how much love we put into the doing. Make sure you know your neighbor, for that knowledge will lead you to great love and love to personal service."[11]

Mother Teresa is famous for affirming repeatedly that our love must go out to the poor—for the love of God. She presented a radical way of living the gospel, one that most of us cannot emulate directly, and her life continues to be an inspiration to spiritual people of all faiths. "Being happy with God means this," she wrote, "to love as he loves, to help as he helps, to give as he gives, to serve as he serves."[12]

This sounds simple but presents us with a great challenge. Each of us works out our own way of answering this call. Perhaps it's not your vocation to work in a soup kitchen or a shelter for the homeless. It's important not to condemn yourself if one particular form of service is not your calling. As you look around the cityscape, you can find so many others, and one will be right for you. Your choice may surprise you.

So it was with one of the West's great painters. Vincent van Gogh (1853–90) serves us to this day with his paintings. "His subjects were not formally religious," writes Robert Ellsberg. "They included sunflowers, wheat fields, and starry night skies, but ultimately his subject was the holiness of existence."[13] Van Gogh originally felt called to be a minister, as was his father, but Vincent did badly in seminary and took his ministry to a community of poor miners and their families. He shared their poverty and preached the gospel—and felt himself to be a failure. "Art became his way of expressing his solidarity and compassion for suffering humanity. As a preacher, he had found that the images of poverty and misery among the miners turned his mind to God. And now through art, he sought to record those impressions." Van Gogh's greatest desire was to create art that touched people. "'I should want my work to show what is in the heart.'"[14]

Is it possible that his paintings could have fed more souls through the ages than his service to the poor miners and their families?

Worthy Words

Words can be a gift we might give to other people, especially in a busy city. Until recently, I've forgotten to be grateful for the gift of sight, for the simple ability to read and write, which I've long taken for granted. When a neighbor told me about Lighthouse International, I began to think about this gift in new ways. Lighthouse is a ministry of reading to and assisting the blind; I'd spent much of my life reading and writing but never shared these common skills with someone who had no sight.

When I decided to volunteer, I was asked first for an interview. I found myself in a small room on a cold day, awaiting a visually impaired person to whom I was assigned. I was uneasy. What if my voice gave out before the two committed hours were up? Would I meet the expectations of the person on her way to this spare room?

Soon, however, my thoughts were diverted from myself as I listened to two blind people conversing in the hall. It was humbling to listen to them discuss when they had lost their vision—one at birth, one at the age of thirty. A man expertly unfolded his cane and cheerfully called out, "Take care now. Later!" As I looked around the reading room where I sat, I noticed a large bowl on the floor. After a moment, I realized that it was the water dish for any guide dog that would enter the room with its owner. Light filtered through the windows. I was overwhelmed with gratitude for the gift of my sight.

I've always loved the story of Bartimaeus (see Mark 10:46–52) and often pictured Jesus healing this roadside blind beggar. Now in a new way I recognized how powerful that moment was.

Soon an attractive blond woman was led toward me. I'll call her Mamie here. She was cheerful and said she looked forward to "hearing" her mail and then the libretto of an opera she had recently attended. She still had some sight, she said, but not enough to be able to read.

So we sat down together with her letters and correspondence, and I was amazed by the unexpected intimacy in going through someone else's mail: bills and reminders, announcements and solicitations, a thank you note. This was the kind of mail I so often scan quickly, sometimes scarcely giving it a glance. I've not been able to do this since reading to Mamie.

Our session in particular showed me the holy in the ordinary. Mamie had set aside sections of the newspaper to hear, and I realized how often I take the daily paper for granted. I was also impressed by Mamie's love of theater. She could still enjoy plays but needed the programs read to her to enhance her enjoyment. I left the session feeling that I was the one being blessed by this woman of courage and grace and gratitude. I like the personal contact that the Lighthouse brings me, and I look forward to my weekly session with Mamie. We laugh together, and it's a very good sound as the winter darkness comes down. We leave each other saying, "Next week! Later!" And I go away with immense gratitude: for sight, for Mamie, and for the Holt sisters—the socialites who wanted to do something meaningful with their lives and founded the Lighthouse.

Meals Ministry

Meals on Wheels, in its various forms and under various names, has become a needed, familiar service in cities. This service delivers thousands of free meals a year to people who are homebound or unable to afford food. The fully prepared meal often brings a friendly visit along with the more tangible fare.

In Washington DC over a decade ago, a friend with AIDS was the recipient of a service called Food and Friends. We were both impressed with the well-cooked, nutritious meal and also with the prompt, caring delivery. For some people, meal delivery is the only human contact of the day, and a touch of divine grace. There are many ways to participate in our cities' various Meals on Wheels programs. We may feel more comfortable preparing the food and cooking the meal. But there are others who choose to be the delivery person and visit the meal's recipient. God has a way of using all of us—and the experience to enrich our souls.

"You know I don't go to any one church," my friend commented. "But this kind of thing says, 'Hey, there *is* a God, and God likes me.'"

Our very presence brings a reminder to us both that God is always present.

In part, this reminder comes from the fact that the gift of nourishment touches such a primal chord. This is the stuff of life, this foil-wrapped package of food in your hands—and an antidote for what Mother Teresa called "the disease" of feeling unwanted. If you choose this form of service, in whatever capacity that feels right, you can cook or deliver good food meditatively, holding the recipient(s) in prayer as you go about the work at hand.

There are other ways of using food as your form of service. I once knew a doctor who felt an emptiness in his life. All week long, he helped sick people. Every Sunday, he went to church. And still, he felt something was missing. When he heard about Rachael's Women's Center, a new light kindled in his eyes. At lunchtime there, home-baked desserts were rare. The doctor, a single man, began baking chocolate-pecan brownies every week for the women of Rachael's, who looked forward to the fresh, hand-made treat.

"I finally *did* something," the doctor told me after his first delivery. There was something awestruck in his voice, as if he could scarcely believe what he had accomplished. "I finally did it," he said again, his eyes bright. The doctor's baking ministry lasted for years.

Virtual Visits

Many urban Meals on Wheels programs have opportunities for regular "telephone visits," which can be made from one's home or office to someone who is homebound. In one city, this may be called Telephone Reassurance; in another, a Senior Chat. Depending on the program, the call is made daily or weekly as a way to check on the recipient's well-being and also as a verbal visit. It's a wonderful way to combat the loneliness that can occur in the city.

You've heard of that and may know about it—the feeling of being isolated and alone even while in the midst of a crowd or bustling metropolitan center. In some cases, perhaps, as people age or their circumstances change, connections break down. You don't know the people who live in the apartment down the hall or overhead, except by the anonymous sounds we hear: a sofa bed unfolded, the hum of plumbing, the tinkling of a piano.

So the telephone visit is a good reminder that another human being knows us and cares about our welfare. Through these calls, a special relationship can gradually grow up over the course of time. There's nothing like the sound of a familiar voice, but apartment building newsletters can also help isolated people keep up with the community, which is so interdependent, so bound together in trust for basic safety and responsibility. When we pray in intercession, we might add all the people under the same roof with us. And while we're praying, we may visit the Web site of www.gratefulness.org, where we may light free online candles for individuals and groups.

Urban hot lines bring the gift of personal presence to a stranger. Cities usually have diverse hot lines that offer a great many services to a wide range of people, and each call can be taken in a quietly prayerful way. My experience on such a hot line was memorable. I worked an evening shift on a weekend, every two weeks. Sometimes the calls were from lonely people who just wanted to talk; others involved crisis situations such as potential suicide.

Cities may have different kinds of hot lines, and there's always expert training for the volunteer before going on the line. Even with the presence of the Internet and chat rooms, there seems to be no substitute for the human voice.

Voice to Voice

Through the hot line, I heard the voices of the lonely, the lost, and the desperate, and I felt the instinct to pray for each one of them rising in direct proportion to my own feelings of helplessness. I still recall the voice of a narcotics police officer who had reached the breaking point. He had just discovered a teenager with a heroin syringe in her eye. The officer broke down, then couldn't stop talking. Other hot line volunteers listened to him throughout the night until he was in safe territory again, or so we hoped. There was never any way of knowing for sure.

Hot line calls are humbling. They made me realize again, with force, how small I was and how unequal to so many of the problems that came through the telephone line. We were trained in reflective listening, not problem solving, and it was important to be mindful that there is a power in simply being with a troubled person, even if we lack the power or authority to "fix" the problem. A spiritual life is an important undergirding for this kind of service.

I'll always remember the woman who ran a fine shelter and was my mentor there for many years. She taught me as much by example as by speech. I learned small things from her: never give money, always own a first aid kit, wash your hands, say a silent prayer before you speak.

"You need a faith life if you're going to help people," she said once. "You need to know that you're not the only one doing the helping. When you turn out the light and go home, God is still there, working, watching, and God never sleeps."

And There Is More

People who do craftwork often organize to do acts of service. Chemo Caps, for example, is a group of knitters that donates its time by creating caps for cancer patients on hospital oncology wards. The Knitting Guild of America sponsors the Precious Pals Program to provide comfort to children in crisis. This group provides thousands of stuffed animals to police departments all over the United States. You can find these organizations online; you can also use the Internet to find ways to serve incarcerated persons too. You can't call such people, but you can send them books, which widen what for many is a narrowed world.

Prison libraries are busy and valued places; an inspiring friend of mine worked at one for years before starting a prison parenting program, and she stresses the power of the written word in correctional settings.

You can send books through several organizations, among them Books Behind Bars, in Philadelphia (www.writeaprisoner.com/books-behind-bars) or to Women's Prison Book Project in Minneapolis (www.prison activist.org/wpbp). Kairos Prison Ministry also helps volunteers connect more directly, and with supervision, with incarcerated persons.

Correspondence with prisoners is another way to serve people who usually feel stigmatized and isolated. My prison pen pal is a caring person who works in her institution's school and reads mysteries and reaches beyond herself to ask about my health and well-being. It's wise, however, to have a social worker, chaplain, or prison school principal refer you to the incarcerated who are open to correspondence.

A superb book of resources (complete with Web addresses) is *One Good Work at a Time: Simple Things You Can Do to Make a Difference* by Frances Sheridan Goulart. She divides her book in ways that help us sort through the plentiful options that are available to us: through prayer, in the home, in the workplace, in the community, in society, in the environment, and in the global community.

Goulart begins with a quote from Psalm 37: "Trust in the LORD, and do good." She follows that with an early Christian saying, *Nobis es,* from the Latin meaning "it's up to us."[15]

And so it is.

"Doing God's work is an equal opportunity ministry to which we are all called," writes Goulart. "Opportunities to be God's hand, eyes, and ears in the world for the greater good are all around us.... Giving unconditional love because we are first loved by him who created us helps to restore our sense of belonging, our recognition that humankind is one big family."[16]

When we achieve this recognition in a big, busy city, we live out our faith and enrich our spirituality.

_____◁◇◇◇▷_____

*I will bless the LORD at all times: his praise shall continually be
    in my mouth.*
*My soul shall make her boast in the LORD: the humble shall hear
    thereof, and be glad.*
O magnify the LORD with me, and let us exalt his name together.
*I sought the LORD, and he heard me, and delivered me from all
    my fears.*
*They looked unto him, and were lightened: and their faces were
    not ashamed.*
*This poor man cried, and the LORD heard him, and saved him
    out of all his troubles....*
*The LORD is nigh unto them that are of a broken heart; and
    saveth such as be of a contrite spirit. (Psalm 34:1–6, 18)*

CURES FOR *Soulsickness*
IN THE CITY

Stop: Read and Receive

1. How does your service to others reflect your commitment to God? How do you see God in those whom you serve?

2. How do you practice charity? Do you prefer to put aside a bit of money each week, or do you prefer to give your time (and to what, where, how)? How can you begin to do both?

3. When have you ever practiced service or charity anonymously? How have you ever given money, goods, time, or service to people who cannot give back?

4. Do you consider rude people as those to whom you can give patience and time? Is a refrain from reproof a sign of service or victimhood?

Yield: Reflect, Journal, or Discuss

5. How are you able to serve without patronizing the recipients? How can you find a way to follow the example of Jesus as He washed the feet of His disciples?

6. Jot down some notes or journal about a time you were mindful of the varied and vast opportunities for urban service. Reflect upon or discuss with a friend how aware you are that all spiritual traditions believe that service, in some form, is asked of us by God. Do you believe this? Why or why not? Enough to act on it—and in what ways, when, how?

7. Do you see service as a substitute for prayer or as a part of the spiritual life, alongside prayer? When can your service be a form of prayer? How so?

8. Journal about your attitude toward service. Notice if you serve with a sense of obligation or if you're able to serve with humor and good spirits.

Go: Experience and Engage

9. When you look at a homeless, impaired, or troubled person, how can you identify with him or her? Write on an index card at least three ways or practices you use. If you find yourself stumped on the *how,* stop right now. Ask God to aid you. Pray with a friend for guidance. Now keep trying to think of ways to note on the card, which you can keep in a place you look at frequently for reminders.

10. Think about your city's needs and opportunities and to which ones God is calling you. List areas of service to which you feel called or drawn. Make an action plan with three steps of how to serve your city. The first action step may be to gather information and research a ministry or program. The second action step may be to contact the program or ministry; be sure to set a date and write out your intention. The third action step may be to map out how you can serve and when you'll begin—mark these things on your calendar or in your day planner.

11. Admit with honest humility that you are *not* drawn to every form of service. Set aside a prayer time (daily, weekly)—something designated like a date with God—to seek His leading on this path.

12. Notice when you feel a special connection with someone you've served. Record how you sensed God's presence (or not) before, during, and after the experience.

FINDING GOD IN ALOOFNESS

The Gateway to Mercy

Would you put your hand in my pocket to see if I have my keys?" the elderly woman asked a neighbor in their apartment building's elevator. The keys were in her pocket, but in the lobby the woman forgot this and had to ask a doorman to check again for her keys.

A presentable woman, she clung to her independence and some semblance of normal life, even with impaired health. Family and caregivers visited her, and she often liked to stand in the lobby, looking out at the busy city. But when this woman wandered outside the lobby, even a few feet onto the sidewalk, she was often treated with impatience, irritation, or indifference.

In the same city, about twenty blocks north, on an upscale avenue of boutiques and galleries, a somewhat similar drama recently unfolded.

The owner of an antiques gallery decided to sue a homeless man for sitting on a steam grate near the gallery. Several neighboring store owners sympathized with the antiques dealer. The lawsuit against the homeless man was for a million dollars.

On another busy street, a pedestrian paused to get her bearings. She felt a small but distinct shove: someone's forefinger between her shoulder blades. "Move it, will ya?" a young man blurted as he pushed past her. The young man, in turn, was nearly grazed by a messenger, who did not apologize. "Don't walk behind me," a stranger abruptly commanded another pedestrian.

Nearby, a soft-spoken woman tentatively approached an idling, empty taxi. "Are you available, sir?" she asked the cab driver who was hunched over the steering wheel. Exasperated, he turned, shouting, "Ya see anyone in the back seat?" She shook her head. "Ya see my light's on?" She nodded. "Then whaddya waiting for?" Speechless, she got in the taxi just as someone else grabbed the door handle on the other side.

Days later, I sat at a sidewalk table of an open-front Italian restaurant on a busy street. I sipped my tea, awaiting a friend, and watched the pedestrians moving past me. A young man, walking a golden retriever, had just cleaned up after his pet as required by city law. He spied me at my table and, grinning suddenly, he held up his filled, clear plastic doggy bag and shook it at me. "Have a nice lunch," he laughed. Before I could speak, he was gone.

That's Tough

Urban people, it's often said, have to be tough to survive in a competitive, high-stakes, fast-moving world. But is this necessarily so?

After the terrorist attacks of September 11, 2001, there was a great outpouring of compassion and self-giving in New York City's and Washington DC's metropolitan areas. Other cities sent aid in many forms, including whole fire departments. There was a similar response from our cities when Hurricane Katrina devastated New Orleans. This enhanced sense of compassion seemed to last for quite a while…and yet within just a few years of each incident this merciful stance seems to be diminishing.

A cartoon from the *New Yorker* offers a witty warning about the shift taking place. In the cartoon, two women are walking down a Manhattan street. One woman tells the other, "It's hard, but slowly I'm getting back to hating everyone."[1]

This attitude, however it's lampooned, is one of the shadow sides of city living. To ignore the shadow would be naive indeed, just as it would be unrealistic to ignore the presence of urban crime chronicled in the local news every day—violence, violation, and vice.

In major metropolitan business districts, toughness may turn into ruthlessness. Toughness may also turn into insensitivity to others, as in the case of the elderly lady who kept thinking she had lost her keys. We may be impatient not only with the marginalized but with strangers in our midst. In a high-pressure urban environment, it's easy to be curt when asked for directions or merely the time of day.

Toughness, of course, exists everywhere. But city living seems to bring it out a bit more. Sometimes I feel defensive on rainy urban streets: umbrellas clash, the pace grows even faster, cars splash pedestrians, people sometimes vie for space on the sidewalk.

When there are so many people in a relatively small urban locale, we must look out for ourselves, to an extent. This is a spiritual challenge: living out God's mercy under such circumstances. On rainy streets, as we dodge the dueling spokes of umbrellas, we may find it easy to forget that God is present with us: immanent, real, and seeking us, right here where we are.

I saw a reminder of this just last night. It was bitterly cold and windy at a busy midtown intersection. Laden with many packages, a woman and child were trying to hail a cab. But cabs were few and filled. About twenty feet away, a well-heeled couple dressed for a formal evening out was also attempting to flag down a taxi. At last one stopped—bypassing the mother and selecting the couple. Without hesitation, the pair summoned the mother and child, picked up their packages, and put them all in the taxi. I am still haunted by the shivering child's face as it broke into a smile. God's mercy seemed almost tangibly present on that cold corner.

Love Knocking

Charles H. Spurgeon, the great nineteenth-century preacher, told the story of a minister calling on a poor woman in order to help her. When he knocked on her door, however, no one answered. The minister, assuming the woman was out, later happened upon her at his church. She apologized for not answering the door, explaining she feared the knock was from the rent collector.[2]

How freely God gives us love, and how often we are suspicious of it—perhaps more so in cities.

"We may like to think of ourselves as people who are seeking God, but the Bible is very clear that it is really the other way around," writes Albert Holtz in *Downtown Monks: Sketches of God in the City.* "It is God who is constantly seeking us. Every page of sacred Scripture shows a God in love, a God passionately pursuing the human heart. From the biblical point of view, then, our main task is to let ourselves be caught and wrapped up in the Lord's loving embrace."[3]

The prophet Hosea shows us this God, the God who woos back a people that has strayed, just as a good husband would seek the return of an unfaithful wife.

Throughout the gospels, God in Christ nurtures multitudes of people through countless acts of mercy. You read of healing, forgiving, teaching, feeding. Jesus stretches out His hand to the blind, the lame, and the suffering wherever He goes. At the tomb of Lazarus, Jesus weeps. In a parable of God's kingdom, Jesus encourages us to invite the marginalized to our most lavish feasts (see Luke 14:13).

No, God is not shy or embarrassed to refer to the word *heart.*

Mellow Hearts

In *The Holy Longing,* Ronald Rolheiser stresses "mellowness of heart" as one of the four pillars of a healthy spirituality. The pillars, he says, are what hold our faith up and support it; the other pillars are service, prayer, and worship.[4]

It may be unfair to say, but I think it's true that mellowness of heart is not often associated with urban living. And yet, one of the West's most beloved stories takes place in a city and involves the heart's conversion. You remember *A Christmas Carol*, set in nineteenth-century London. Is it a fairy tale that the central character, the cold-hearted miser Ebenezer Scrooge, has isolated himself from others and feels no mercy for them until the Christmas Eve when he's shown a panorama of his spiritually impoverished life?

I think not. I am always moved by the shaken and remorseful Scrooge rushing about his city that Christmas Day, doing good and filling his remaining years with generosity, kindness, and joy.[5]

The softening of a hard heart is seldom quite that simple, and yet Scrooge's story remains one of our favorites, perhaps because it shows us the power of conversion and the image of who we might become. I need to hear such stories. They inspire me and get me back on track. *A Christmas Carol* reminds me to look at the big picture, in the midst of busy city life, and reflect on God's mercy.

I like Scrooge's story for another reason too. It takes a clear-eyed look at the way most of us can be when we're at our worst. The Psalms do this unabashedly: so many of them speak of despair, anger, and struggle. I think of Psalm 22, with its famous cry of dereliction, spoken by Jesus on the cross.

"If this record of a soul's struggle to find God is to be complete," Frank Laubach wrote in his diary in 1930, "it must not omit the story of difficulty and failure. I have not succeeded very well so far. This week, for example, has not been one of the finest in my life, but I resolve not to give up the effort.... At this moment I feel something 'let go inside,' and lo, God is here! It is a heart-melting 'here-ness,' a lovely whispering of father to child, and the reason I did not have it before was because I failed to let go."[6]

A Merciful Meal

I remember watching a homeless woman let go in an urban shelter. It was dinnertime, and I was helping serve stew and rice from huge, steaming vats. Outside, rain was pounding the streets of Washington DC. Many women came to dinner wrapped in plastic bags discarded by dry cleaners. One older woman glared at a volunteer who tried to collect her empty paper plate. There was rage in the her eyes as she growled, "It's mine. This plate—it belongs to me."

The volunteer calmly explained that plates couldn't be taken out of the dining room. The volunteer's voice grew steely and hard.

The homeless woman's voice rose too.

I remember exchanging looks with my fellow server. Would there be a fight? What could be done?

Just then, another woman rose from her table. Taking the situation in at a glance, she approached the older woman and embraced her. The paper plate drifted to the floor. The two women, rocking together now, wept.

We had all witnessed the power of mercy in action and under pressure.

Hard Hearts

In a large city, where we're so pressed and pressured, it's tempting to suppress or diminish the merciful side of our nature. At times I know I've felt less vulnerable when I'm emotionally well defended, and sometimes that means steeling myself when mercy would require courage.

City life, often centered on "striving, on competition, on comparison, can kill our hearts without us even noticing that they are dead," writes Arthur Jeon. "But the true nature of humans yearns to rise above the conditioning that puts them in a state of separation and fear and in competition with each other for a piece of the pie."[7]

The Scriptures warn against such hardness of heart, and Jesus echoes God's refrain through the gospels (see Matthew 19:8). In the beloved Psalm 95 we're urged, "To day if ye will hear his voice, harden not your heart" (verses 7–8).

In fact, that plea is often the first line chanted by contemplatives in the earliest hour of communal prayer.

In the gospel of Luke, Jesus tells two parables that contrast mellow hearts with hard ones. In the parable of the prodigal son, already mentioned, the older brother's heart is hardened in resentment against his brother, while his father's heart is forgiving, open, and warm. And in the parable of the good Samaritan, we again see a person showing compassion for a broken man lying beside a highway (leading to the large city of Jericho). The rescuer is probably an urban merchant of different ethnicity who aids the victim after the overtly righteous pass by. Perhaps we all know that we could easily be that wounded man—and just as easily, the busy people of the world who ignored him (see Luke 10:30–36).

These two parables are well known among people of many faiths and are among the most beloved stories in the Bible. They touch a common chord in us and show us, if not who we are, who we might be—and even what's possible in our cities, highways, and very world too.

The great liberation theologian Gustavo Gutiérrez wrote about such possibilities and warm-heartedness—components of a healthy spirituality. He said such a spirituality includes prayer and social justice and is always balanced with the feeling, caring heart. Justice, paired with love, he said, could truly change our lives, our cities, and our world.[8]

Heartening Words

As we grow in spirituality, suggests M. Basil Pennington, our consciousness tends to be transformed. The process is different for every person, and the common key is regular prayer that transforms the external life as well as the interior self.

Prayer isn't an easy escape, Pennington taught, nor is it a way to find quick bliss in the time we set aside for centering on God each day. Rather, "this return to the Center, this embrace of God is the sourcing of life, the transformation of life, the birth of compassion leading to another whole way of living. The choices we make in centering prayer follow through into life."[9]

I still feel gentled by my own experience with centering prayer. Sometimes when I begin, my mind jumps around like an insect and moves at a very fast pace. On occasion, disturbing thoughts surface at this beginning time: mistakes, missteps, injuries, insults—some recent, some from years before. Then, as I keep returning my attention to God, I slow down and the mist of brokenness seems to lift. I emerge from these periods feeling more tender, more patient, more blessed and grateful; I've somehow been renewed by God, through this prayer discipline.

Pennington's words are true for me: "As we come to know by experience of the Center our oneness with each and every person, and also the potential goodness and happiness that is available to fill the life of each, we enter more and more into the compassion of Christ.... We love more deeply and more universally."[10]

My prayers are still works in progress, and in process, as I know they will always be. There are times when I can go deep in the centering prayer that Pennington describes, and the fruits are as he explains. And there are other times when I can only pray for mercy.

Having Mercy

Doesn't that word *mercy* have a religious ring to it? It's interesting to note that this word is also related to commerce—the very root of *mercy* is from the Latin for "price paid; wages," and from the French, *merx,* for merchandise, according to *Webster's Collegiate Dictionary.* Our modern word *mercy,* then, has an urban mercantile connotation rather than an ecclesiastical one. A merchant who forgives a debt is acting out of mercy, for example.

In current usage, synonyms for mercy are charity, clemency, grace, and leniency.

"Mercy implies compassion that forbears punishing, even when justice demands it," *Webster's* tells us. It's seen in the same light as "a disposition to show kindness" and "a benign attitude and a willingness to grant favors or concessions," especially to others who may be in our power.[11]

Mercy was an important concept in biblical times, when the prophets preached in cities and Jesus preached in cities and towns. Scripturally, mercy is one of the foremost ways to describe the nature of God. There are about a hundred references to God's mercy in the Psalms (Psalm 107:1, for example: "his mercy endureth for ever") composed by King David in the city of Jerusalem. The mercy of God pervades the Hebrew Scriptures.

God's call for our own mercy is frequent: "For I desired mercy, and not sacrifice" (Hosea 6:6).

In the gospels, mercy is given great emphasis and divine mercy invites our response. "Blessed are the merciful," Jesus teaches in the Sermon on the Mount (Matthew 5:7), "for they shall obtain mercy." In the gospel of Luke, Jesus calls us to be merciful, "as your Father also is merciful" (6:36), and James 5:11 describes God as "very pitiful, and of tender mercy."

Mercy, then, is part of our heritage on many levels, from the Judeo-Christian faith tradition to the commercial legacy we have from medieval marketplaces in town centers. In times of urban disaster—power outages, strikes, and notably during war, natural disasters, and terrorist attacks—mercy seems to spring forth, unbidden, from within a city and from its sister metropolises.

Through a mindful attitude toward mercy, urban people practice it more quietly, less dramatically, perhaps, on a daily basis—in "ordinary time," when their city is not directly threatened by catastrophe, such as Hurricane Katrina's devastation of New Orleans, or the horror of 9/11 in Manhattan, or, a century ago, the San Francisco earthquake.

How can we practice mercy more often in our daily urban lives?

How about taking a breath in that moment when you might otherwise yell at a screaming motorist? Or stop yourself from pushing back when someone on the street shoves you or tells you to "move it." How about giving the pedestrian the right of way, along with the person walking a collision course on a busy avenue? Or engaging in the practice of the ancient church called *statio*—using the "stops" in our day to remember the idea of mercy, the notion of "mellowness of heart."

You can take it further, as did a member of a neighboring synagogue when the antiques dealer sued the homeless man, previously mentioned, for a million dollars. The synagogue member came to sit on the grate that the homeless man (now frightened away) had occupied. This visitor was not demonstrating; he simply wanted to know what it felt like to keep warm on a steam grate in a city street. His act was one of genuine empathy.

Misery and Mercy

In sophisticated cities all over the world, a certain play has captivated immense audiences: the dramatization of Victor Hugo's masterpiece *Les Misérables*. Published in Paris in 1862, *Les Misérables* reappeared as a musical play in 1985 in another urban venue: London. From there productions have traveled to most major American cities as well as Tokyo, Berlin, Helsinki, Dublin, Melbourne, and others. While *Les Misérables* isn't about sophisticated urban life, modern manners, style, or commerce, much of the story's action is set in a Paris slum. This play, and its originating novel, is about mercy and redemption. The entire plot, in fact, turns on the concept of mercy.

Jean Valjean, in early-nineteenth-century Paris, is released from prison after a stay of nineteen years, initially for stealing a loaf of bread. At first, Valjean is bitter and angry. When a kindly bishop takes him in for the night, the newly freed man takes the clergyman for a fool—and steals his silver.

The next morning, when Valjean is arrested for the theft, he is shocked to hear the bishop tell the police that no theft took place. Instead, the cleric insists, he has given the silver to the stranger as a gift. Then, privately, the bishop tells Valjean that he must use the silver to start again, to become an honest man. Valjean is profoundly moved by this act of mercy. It changes his entire life—and the lives of those around him.

The reception of this drama has been overwhelmingly enthusiastic wherever it's performed. *Les Misérables* strikes a chord with the amazing range of urban audiences. The story shows how deeply human beings, however modern, however sophisticated, respond to the theme of mercy.

We can do even more than welcome this theme on city stages across the globe; we can make this happen in quiet ways. Like Jean Valjean, we may struggle to open ourselves to mercy, but like Victor Hugo's famous character, we can do this. And perhaps our acts of mercy may affect someone else, as it happens in the story of *Les Misérables,* or in a private, unseen, undramatic way.

Other *"Misérables"*

John Newton, author of the famous hymn "Amazing Grace," has a life story that also turns on a sudden flash of mercy. Many of us know that Newton, who grew up in early-nineteenth-century England, began as a rebellious soul and in his youth went to sea. He then worked hands-on in the slave trade and trafficked in the sale and transport of human beings. Newton captained several slave ships that brought human cargo to American shores.

However, during a great storm at sea, it seemed that one of Newton's ships would go down, and soon. There was nothing he could do as captain to save the vessel. In his autobiographical writings, Newton notes that at that moment, he threw up his hands and cried out, "Then, Lord, have mercy." He then went into his cabin, shut the door, and reflected on what he had just said.

A radical change in Newton's life began then and there.

The ship did not sink, nor did the captain turn it around, as popular legend portrays this conversion of soul. But from that time, Newton's life was gradually transformed. Eventually he became an Anglican curate, ministering to others; in this way he lived the second half of his life, dwelling in a parsonage's small room, where he wrote these famous verses and others:

> Amazing grace, how sweet the sound,
> That saved a wretch like me!
> I once was lost but now I'm found,
> Was blind but now I see.
>
> Through many trials, toils and snares,
> We have already come.
> 'Tis grace that led us here thus far
> And grace will lead us home.[12]

Newton also assisted the famed English abolitionist William Wilberforce in his crusade to end slavery in Great Britain. The former slave trader's inside experience in his onetime profession provided Wilberforce with invaluable information and ammunition for the abolitionist cause. And so, Newton turned his time as a self-proclaimed wretch to the advantage of the people he had once abused.

The hymn "Amazing Grace" is a kind of spiritual autobiography, written with almost painful sincerity; it's inspired a wide range of humanity, from rural congregations in America's Smoky Mountains to the Boys Choir of Harlem, from Judy Collins to Jesseye Norman and Joan Baez. This legacy is ours because John Newton opened his experiences and his spirit to us, and because in the midst of a storm he opened his life to God's mercy.

Newton's story reminds me of Francis Thompson's "The Hound of Heaven." In this ode, the poet flees God throughout his troubled life, until at last, in a spiritual awakening, he turns to embrace the Holy One. This poem is another form of spiritual autobiography, and it never would have reached us if not for two acts of urban mercy.

Merciful Intervention

Born in 1859 near the large city of Manchester, England, Francis Thompson was a restless young man, unsuited to the careers selected for him by his parents: the priesthood, medicine, commerce, and military service. Thompson, instead, wanted to be a poet. Working as a London bookseller, he also became addicted to opium, and this quickly used up his salary.[13]

Although he was educated and cultured, Thompson slid into the life of the homeless on the city's streets. By day, he tried to sell pencils and matches; by night, he slept along the Thames River or under the arches of London's bridges. He very nearly took his own life.

For a time, he was saved by the merciful intervention of a woman who took him in and for whom he later wrote a sonnet. While staying with this woman, Thompson sent a handful of poems to Wilfred Maynell, editor of London's *Merry England* magazine. Eventually, Maynell summoned Thompson to his offices; the editor remembers Thompson opening the door, then closing it, then opening it again, while the bedraggled poet hesitated, "frightened to come in."[14]

"We can only imagine the terror Francis Thompson experienced," writes his biographer, Robert Waldron. "How much courage it must have cost him to arrive at the *Merry England* office, dressed in rags, poorer looking than the average beggar, with no shirt beneath his coat and bare feet in broken shoes and to stand before the impeccably dressed Victorian gentleman and editor Wilfred Maynell. But Maynell was a kind and compassionate man; disregarding appearances, his eyes penetrated to the man beneath the rags."[15]

A long friendship began that night because of Wilfred Maynell's mercy. He helped Francis Thompson regain his health, saw to his treatment for addiction, and moved him to lodgings near his own home. In addition, he employed Thompson as a book reviewer. But Maynell, a man of deep spirituality, never seemed to see himself as the good Samaritan that he was.

Although Thompson again succumbed to cycles of addiction and withdrawal, Maynell remained his staunch friend, periodically sending the poet to a monastery in Sussex, where he struggled while he recovered from a bout with laudanum. It was there that he wrote his famous spiritual poem "The Hound of Heaven," which confesses his struggles to accept God's love:

I fled Him, down the nights and down the days;
I fled Him, down the arches of the years;
I fled Him, down the labyrinthine ways
     Of my own mind; and in the mist of tears
I hid from Him.[16]

But the poet is still hounded by his divine pursuer, until finally the author realizes that it is God whose faithful love is always behind him. The poem ends with God's merciful voice, inviting him home: "Rise, clasp My hand, and come."[17]

The Two of Hearts

For many of us, the presence of mercy is not so dramatic, but it's there, especially if we bring our own small mercies into the rush of city living.

That means letting go of petty disputes more often; asking for the gift of mercy for ourselves and *through* ourselves in prayer; letting the more aggressive person have the taxi or the sales clerk or the broad stretch of the sidewalk. It may even mean starting a mercy discussion group, Bible study, or simple conversation with a friend.

I remember thinking that this concept was too intimate to discuss at all. But many years ago, I sat in an urban church with a group of people learning about Western spirituality. Most of us knew quite a lot about its history and practice, but few of us had experienced the applied spirituality of mercy that challenged us that night.

The leader of the group set a large bowl of roses in the center of the circle we formed. The roses had been rescued from a cathedral garden that very afternoon, before a frost could kill the flowers. This, we were reminded, was an act of mercy. As we focused on the pale, tattered roses floating in that copper bowl, we were invited to reflect on mercy itself: Where did we find it missing from our lives? Where could we be more present to it? So many years later, these are questions many of us still ask ourselves.

Then we were invited to go into small groups and sit in a chair opposite another person. Immediately, the atmosphere changed. We became more guarded, self-protective; we felt more threatened. Was this going to be one of those exercises where embarrassing details had to be revealed in a group setting? We need not have worried.

One person asked the question, "Who are you?" The person opposite would say something like, "I'm a writer," or, "I'm a daughter," or, "I'm a wife." After each reply, the questioner would speak only one phrase: "God is merciful."

At first, the answers were predictable and safe:

"Who are you?"

"A child of God."

"God is merciful… Who are you?"

"A teacher."

"God is merciful… Who are you?"

"A father."

As this ritual went on, the answers grew more revealing. I marveled at the honest responses to the consistent question:

"Who are you?"

"A sinner."

"God is merciful."

The steadiness of that response, no matter what we said, has stayed with me for two decades.

In the great and teeming city of London, between 1596 and 1598, William Shakespeare wrote immortal words about mercy. These words are spoken still by any actress who plays the character of Portia whenever the towering play *The Merchant of Venice* is performed:

> The quality of mercy is not strain'd,
> It droppeth as the gentle rain from heaven
> Upon the place beneath: it is twice blest;
> It blesseth him that gives and him that takes.…
> It is an attribute to God himself;
> And earthly power doth then show likest God's
> When mercy seasons justice.
> —William Shakespeare, *The Merchant of Venice*, Act 4, Scene 1

My soul, wait thou only upon God; for my expectation is from him.
*He only is my rock and my salvation: he is my defence; I shall not
    be moved.*
*In God is my salvation and my glory: the rock of my strength,
    and my refuge, is in God.*

Trust in him at all times; ye people, pour out your heart before him: God is a refuge for us. (Psalm 62:5–8)

———⊗⊗⊗———

God be merciful unto us, and bless us; and cause his face to shine upon us; Selah.
That thy way may be known upon earth, thy saving health among all nations.
Let the people praise thee, O God; let all the people praise thee.
O let the nations be glad and sing for joy: for thou shalt judge the people righteously, and govern the nations upon earth. Selah….
God shall bless us; and all the ends of the earth shall fear him. (Psalm 67:1–4, 7)

CURES FOR *Soulsickness*
IN THE CITY

Stop: Read and Receive

1. How can you be a savvy city person and still have "heart"? On some level, do you ever see a dichotomy between street smarts and spirituality? How so or how not?

2. Do you ever buy into the stereotype that city people are too tough, quick, and sophisticated to be feeling, caring people?

3. Seriously contemplate the Beatitudes of Jesus. Do you agree that the merciful are blessed? Why would Jesus say this?

Yield: Reflect, Journal, or Discuss

4. Spend a set period of time reflecting on Paul's famous statement to the Corinthians about love (1 Corinthians 13). What does this mean for you? Write a mission statement based on your thoughts.

5. Focus on the merciful nature of God. Do you notice any resistance to this aspect of the Holy One? How so or how not?

6. Read the parable of the prodigal son in Luke 15:11–32. Do you identify most with the wastrel son, whose father is so merciful, or the indignant, dutiful older brother? In what ways? Describe these in a notebook or journal or in discussion with a friend.

7. Dr. Wayne Dyer encourages his readership and audiences to care more about being kind rather than being right. What do you think of this idea? For you, does this seem congruent with your work and city setting? In what ways? Write down your thoughts on this or discuss them with a friend.

8. In the Sermon on the Mount, Jesus said, "Blessed are the peacemakers," as well as "the merciful" (Matthew 5:9, 7). What do you think He means? How is this sort of peace-making something you can bring into your soul with the reality of life in the city?

Go: Experience and Engage

9. Today, forgive a debt, an insult, a slight.
10. Today, refuse to work such long hours that it costs you on the relational level at home, with friends, and with God.
11. Today, refuse to cut off other drivers or pedestrians, push your way forward, or grab sale items. Take note of when you're tempted to do these things (or actually do them) and reflect upon these moments in prayer. Ask yourself now: Do I feel humble or self-righteous? In what ways? How can I move toward humility? List three ideas and act on at least one.
12. Today, in a specially appointed time with God, pray for His grace to make you more and more like the father in the parable of the prodigal son.

10

FINDING GOD
IN ISOLATION
The Gateway to Community

I feel as if I have no skin," said the young woman at the end of the table. "I mean, I just feel so vulnerable."

"Believe me," replied an older woman in the hospital's conference room, "you're not alone."

Several other women offered reassurance, and slowly the room seemed to brighten and expand around us. These women were members of a breast cancer support group, and it was my privilege to help them write about their experiences. I was apprehensive at first, since I was the only one in the room who never had breast cancer...and yet we became a special community in that institutional setting.

The room where we met actually began to seem like a chapel to me. It was amazing. We were in a busy hospital on the edge of our nation's capital; the group wasn't overtly religious. But as we laughed and cried and shared our stories, something holy graced us all. And the lesson was clear: spiritual communities take many forms in all kinds of hustling, bustling urban settings.

The Welcome of Church

City churches and urban houses of worship bear powerful testimony to society. "It is as...a house of God," I read in a recent article, "that the church makes its witness. It needs to be present as all of the things that housing means to people: a sanctuary, a shelter, a haven, a refuge, a protected womb, an ark to carry us through the storm."[1]

But this is not the image most of us have when we think of urban centers. Too often, too many of us see cities as highly secular. Soul-less. City dwellers are perceived as isolated and anonymous, and the pristine, white churches of small-town America seem far away from the modern metropolis. Here, houses of worship have so much to compete with: shops, movies, restaurants, and health clubs. And here, myriad social problems threaten to override the church: crowding, crime, grime, homelessness, addiction. And yet, urban spiritual communities meet these challenges in a variety of ways.

The People of God

"Can you really find spiritual community in a city?" one friend asked dubiously. "Cities are so impersonal."

"I don't like the architecture of *that* church," an acquaintance commented, unasked. "It's cold."

Oddly enough, when I think of "that" church, with its contemporary architecture, it isn't the building's structure that I see. It's the warmth of the congregation, the sense of unity that comes at communion, the smile of the pastor. It's reaffirmed for me that one can indeed find spiritual communities in cities.

Sacred space, with all its power and importance, its aesthetics and atmosphere, is naturally important. Community, however, is more than the physical place. By definition, community is a unified body of individuals;

in the Judeo-Christian tradition, for thousands of years, we've seen our-selves as "the people of God."

This tradition goes back to a ragtag band of slaves who were drawn into unity and led out of bondage as God's people. Moses, speaking at the command of God, ordered the Egyptian Pharaoh to release God's people from bondage (see Exodus 5:1). And the Hebrew people were no longer slaves: they belonged to God, openly and clearly.

In the gospels, a similar ragtag band of people followed Jesus, even into desert places where there was nothing for them to eat. Nothing, that is, until the famous miracle of the multiplied loaves and fishes (see Mark 8:1–8). It's noteworthy that God relates to His people as "*Abba*, Father," feeding and nurturing and freeing. Both Old and New Testaments show God worshiped in solitude, but inescapably, also, in community.

Peter's first letter expresses this sense of calling that people feel as God's chosen ones. That calling doesn't come from desire for elitism or snobbery. "Shew forth the praises of him who hath called you out of darkness into his marvellous light," Peter said, "which in time past were not a people, but now are the people of God" (2:9–10).

In the city, it's immensely comforting and challenging to be so called: to belong to God and to belong to one another in God's name. There are so many metropolitan churches that live out this calling, it's impossible to name them all here. Many of these churches started from humble roots or endured catastrophe or have rebounded from attenuation due to a period of movement toward the suburbs. And yet, these spiritual communities remain a people who refuse to relinquish their calling.

In Washington DC, a Lutheran church sits in a neighborhood that's begun to deteriorate. Despite the urban blights of crime and drugs, this church has reached out to its immediate neighbors and a large homeless population. Its shelter for women is the chapel, with mattresses spread on the floor.

One night, I stood in that chapel and held the map for the place-ment of the mattresses. I thought it notable how each one had its place and how each woman who slept in each place liked to know she had her own familiar space, however small.

As the chapel quietly filled, I studied the room: the altar, the hotplate for the coffee pot, a large banner lovingly made of felt that read "I Am the Vine, You Are the Branches." I thought of all the churches, like that one, that invite those in need, those whom Christ said were the equivalent of Himself. I thought of how those who want to give need those who are willing to receive, and how those who receive give to those who give. And I was struck by how the vine, with its branches, still grows in churches and cities all over the world.

Community as Witness

As the homeless and the well heeled alike gather in churches and houses of worship, I'm reminded of the natural human craving for beauty too—something to lift our eyes and our spirits. The creators of the great cathedrals knew this and made their holy buildings into beautiful magnets that draw us still.

Today, in fact, among the sterile office buildings, garbage trucks, and slums of the cities, houses of worship are a striking witness to the power of beauty.

I've recently seen these words in action. In a midtown church, I attended a bilingual Mass that worked seamlessly with passages alternating in English and Spanish, each language enriching the other. The music complemented the Mass, which was a living example of unity in diversity.

Earlier, I was moved by visiting foreign choirs in a contemporary mainstream church, which is carved out of space in a high-rise complex. No church could look more urban, more diverse, and yet be more unified in community. And there it was, open to anyone and everyone, a rich and living witness to urban community.

Storefront Churches

Wedged between bars and bodegas, storefront churches stand out from grittier streets. These hand-painted sanctuaries, from Harlem to

Richmond, St. Louis to Seattle, are a noticeable phenomenon in the city: small, humble, sometimes makeshift—a far cry from the suburban megachurch.

Lily of the Valley Spiritual Church in Chicago is such a storefront sanctuary. Others like it tend to spring up in low-income neighborhoods and immigrant communities, often in abandoned offices, manufacturing centers, and shops. These churches offer worship, social services, family, and hope. Typically, there's upbeat music and worship from the heart, often Pentecostal, and preachers don't have traditional ordination patterns. The spirituality in this setting is inclusive, emotive, and joyous.

The storefront church "is a presence on that street in a building that [otherwise] would be abandoned," Camilo Jose Vergara observes in his book *How the Other Half Worships.* To me, this shows true soul in the city, a community unwilling to give over even a part of the city to soul-lessness, a community that says, in Vergara's words, "We're alive! The neighborhood may be disappearing.... Many other houses are boarded up. The factories certainly left a long time ago. But we are still here."[2]

There's an inclusive spirituality in the storefront church, one that embraces all forms of brokenness in a personal way. Evelyn Atwood at Lily of the Valley Spiritual Church in Chicago says, "We're like a family. I wash dishes as much as anybody else, scrub floors." And she teaches.[3]

Michael Griffin of Spirit Redeemed Church in Chicago says, "If you're a prostitute, we have someone who has been that route. If you are a drug addict or drug user, if you were the dealer, we have people whose lives have been changed."[4]

In Manhattan's Harlem, Danilo Florian is a factory worker by day and a pastor by night. His storefront church, Ark of Salvation, is made up mostly of immigrants from the Dominican Republic; there are people from all walks of life—reformed drug dealers, families of prisoners, and people on the poverty line.

"What they share," David Gonzalez observes in the *New York Times,* "is a faith in God, in miracles, and in one another. Religion here is not some sober, introspective journey or Sunday chorus, but a raucous communal celebration that spills throughout the week. People whose lives are as marginal as their neighborhoods discover a joyful intimacy often lacking in big churches." Here they also find assistance for various social needs, and "acceptance and recognition that often elude them on the outside."[5]

These tiny, cramped sanctuaries make me think of the house churches that marked early Christian worship—the house churches in cities from Rome to Corinth to Antioch, where shared faith, shared sacraments, and a sense of extended family were of primary importance—and embraced a wide diversity of peoples.

Rich Diversity

As a small child, I sensed the power of a diverse spiritual community in Manhattan. I remember watching people in a great, vaulted church and thinking how different everyone was and how beautiful they looked, gathered together, in the patterns they made.

I would study the worshipers' hands: the calluses on the workmen's, the rough redness of the housemaids', the elegant manicures of some—black hands, white, brown, tan; some clasped, some open palmed. There were different smells in the nave as well: perfume and perspiration, flowers and dust, tallow and incense, grime and grease and old stone. The blue light spilling through the stained-glass windows seemed to unite all the smells, all the hands, all the bent heads, into one spiritual community.

It didn't occur to me then that these people around me were strangers. Enveloped by the holy hush, we were invisibly, mystically connected. I didn't yet understand theology: the kingdom of God and the body of Christ. But we were part of both in that moment of silent worship between words and music.

Decades later, I encountered that same sense of spiritual community where I least expected to find it: under the harsh, florescent lights of a downtown shelter for homeless women in Washington DC. It was a frigid January evening, Martin Luther King Jr.'s birthday, and the halls were noisy. Even so, a hush had fallen over the women in the shelter's shabby common room, with its sagging couch and wobbly tables.

The women had formed a prayer circle, and they stood, heads bent, not touching, yet connected by the silence and the flickering pattern from the candles in their hands. They offered prayers as they felt moved to do so, and almost every prayer began with thanksgiving—for waking up, for living through another day, for teeth, for hands, for dinner, for a bed. To each prayer, this gathered spiritual community called out, "Amen, sister." Finally one voice began a song, and another voice joined the first, and then others were lifted: jagged voices, on-key, off-key, all singing together in a strange harmony, and the song they sang was "We Shall Overcome."

Song. Light. Food. Home. These are the things churches and the church community offer cities. Are they Band-Aids on larger, complex urban issues?

Some might say so. I think not. I believe something I read: "When people are hurt and bleeding, Band-Aids are better than nothing; that some hope is better than no hope; that a dim sign of God's presence in the city is better than no sign. I rejoice that the urban church is a place where people still gather to share victories and defeats, little successes and quiet achievements. Patching one another's wounds is no small accomplishment."[6]

In the house of God, candles are lit, symbolizing warmth, brightness, hope, and His presence. In church, we hear familiar words and voices; in church, God feeds us—Communion, the Holy Eucharist, is the central act, a sacramental meal.

Passed Over

Though church homes feed the soul, like most homes, there can be dysfunction there too. In cities, where the spiritual witness is so important, there's a higher potential for the bone-chilling loneliness that comes in crowds. It's easy for a seeker or visitor to be overlooked in a large, urban church; too often a stranger sits through a service and afterward isn't greeted or even acknowledged.

I remember sitting in the back of a new church, in a new city, feeling a cloak of shyness fall over me. After worship, I stood, alone, at the edge of the room where coffee was served. No one seemed to notice me standing there with my cup and my pastry. *What am I doing here?* I wondered, missing my church in another city.

Maybe you've had the same thoughts in a similar situation.

Ray Bakke notes in *The Urban Christian:* "Fellowship is the community dimension of congregational life, so gloriously present in the book of Acts. The urban church must function intentionally as a community and as a family."[7]

Strangers must be greeted, welcomed, befriended. In this, there is soul.

"Love for each other," Ray Bakke says, "across racial and class barriers, still remains the most powerful testimony to Jesus Christ and the Gospel."[8]

Biblical Spiritual Communities

The Scriptures show us how to become a spiritual community. The people of Israel worshiped together and as an extended family and fled Egypt to worship God in the wilderness. The focal point became the ark of the covenant, which was also worshiped in community.

Your city can be like a biblical symbol of corporate solidarity, Ray Bakke writes: "A city, namely Jerusalem itself, became a symbol of God's presence and power in the world."[9] And this city, this extended community, was a magnet for spiritual pilgrims who flocked to the great temple at least once a year. "It was clearly taught in the Old Testament that Jerusalem was something special,...the place that God had ordained and where his name would dwell (Deuteronomy 12:11) and even in ruins (Isaiah 44:5, 49:16) affirmations would be made on its behalf."[10]

The gospels repeatedly refer to Jesus's ministry in cities small and large, as well as in the synagogue and the temple. Matthew recorded how "Jesus went about all the cities and villages, teaching in their synagogues, and preaching the gospel of the kingdom, and healing every sickness and every disease among the people" (Matthew 9:35; also noted in Matthew 10:23; 11:1; Mark 6:33, 56; and Luke 13:22). And it's notable: Jesus was born in a small town and made His way to the holy city of Jerusalem—

to teach in the city temple, celebrate the Passover with His own spiritual community, and die on the cross with the multitudes around Him. After the Resurrection, the joyous outpouring of the Holy Spirit at Pentecost was also an urban spiritual occurrence that blessed a widening community.

Before Constantine, early Christians worshiped in Antioch, Corinth, and Rome, in private homes and in the catacombs. Paul was thoroughly urban, and after his mission to many cities, the pattern of urban spiritual communities became firmly established.

Spiritual communities, then, have always been rooted in urban centers—from Jerusalem's temple to Rome's catacombs, from medieval cathedrals to storefront churches. These communities have outlasted wars, plagues, and most recently, flight from cities to suburbs. The urban house of worship is a powerful witness to God's presence among towers of mercantile power, and sometimes amid crime, grime, and poverty.

Great Spiritual Centers

You too may be a pilgrim to a spiritual community, be it a classic medieval cathedral, a storefront church, a historic synagogue, or to the First Corinthians Missionary Baptist Church, founded by an African American community in 1950 in a rickety, abandoned structure. Since then, the church has grown and thrived due to the intensely involved congregation and its charismatic pastors. During its first fifteen years, First Corinthians MBC moved five times, and it has become a strong and spirit-filled community. It is one of thousands of black churches that have originated in urban storefront settings. Since the great migration of African Americans to northern cities, black churches have become powerful spiritual magnets and offer wide-ranging community outreach.[11]

A different kind of spiritual magnet exists on the edge of Harlem in Manhattan: the Intervale Jewish Community Center. The late Moishe Sacks, who ran the center for decades, saw the urban neighborhood as a place "to uncover an image of the city as a space where God was immanent," writes Robert A. Orsi in *Gods of the City: Religion and the American*

Urban Landscape. Urban violence and decay could not overpower this vital spiritual community, whose bricks once reminded Sacks of the great temple of Jerusalem. As members of Intervale pass on, new members keep taking their place.[12]

Another strong spiritual community is the Japanese Presbyterian Church in Seattle (JPC). It too draws upon the ethnic diversity of the urban landscape. With its Japanese architecture and bilingual services, JPC is a thriving church which began as a mission to Japanese immigrants in 1907. One hundred years later, it is an increasingly diverse spiritual center in America's Northwest region. The church windows look out onto a central courtyard and a Japanese garden, conducive to meditation and to "cultivate the beauty of one's inner being and soul," said the Reverend Richard Nishioka, "in an American space with a Japanese flair."[13]

I find it reassuring to discover in the city so many spiritual communities with such great diversity. These are living, tangible witnesses to the fact that city life and spirituality are, indeed, congruent, life giving, and mutually inspiring.

This inspiration is highly valuable. There have always been great challenges facing urban houses of worship. I admire a man who confronted these challenges. Walter Rauschenbusch was an advocate of the Social Gospel in the United States. Rauschenbusch was also a pastor at a Baptist church in New York City's Hell's Kitchen, a community afflicted with poverty, disease, and despair. In response to this situation, Rauschenbusch tried "to awaken the conscience of the church to its responsibilities in the world."

In 1891, he began to focus on "the biblical symbol of the kingdom of God, the central message that Jesus had proclaimed. It was an all encompassing theme that included personal faith and social transformation."[14] To me this means that our worship together extends beyond liturgy. This worship can also take the form of ministry to the hungry, the homeless, the broken. This is the kingdom of God as Jesus revealed it.

Today, we are still challenged to live out this vision. "The vision of life in the kingdom, through reliance upon Jesus, makes it possible for us to *intend* to live in the kingdom, as he did," writes Dallas Willard. "We can intentionally *decide to do it.*"[15] But how does that look to us in our urban worlds? Again, we begin small—with prayer, worship, service, and mercy—and we do it together.

Why Community?

We have received an extraordinary promise from God, a promise which emerges as daring, as stunning, when we reflect on it: "For where two or three are gathered together in my name, there am I in the midst of them" (Matthew 18:20).

Jesus ministered with a small community of disciples around Him and usually ministered to groups. Rick Warren, in *The Purpose-Driven Life,* gives these examples as the biblical invitation to spiritual community. "Only the Holy Spirit can create real fellowship between believers, but he cultivates it with the choices and commitments we make. Paul points out this dual responsibility when he urges us to be, 'endeavoring to keep the unity of the Spirit in the bond of peace' (Ephesians 4:3)."[16]

Many contemporary people do not see community as a context for authentic spirituality—for them, an individual spiritual life is preferable. I understand this: I am not a "joiner" by nature. And yet I have always been drawn to a worshiping community. As Warren points out, in genuine fellowship, "people experience mercy. Fellowship is a place of grace." We all need mercy, he asserts, and in a true spiritual community, mercy abides.[17]

"Life is meant to be shared," writes Warren. "God intends for us to experience life together. The Bible calls this shared experience *fellowship....* Real fellowship is so much more than showing up at services.... It includes unselfish loving, honest sharing, practical serving, sacrificial giving, sympatric comforting."[18]

I've seen this happen many times. At one parish during Lent, people in small groups went out to serve the larger city community. At another, a visitors committee sent parishioners to shut-ins and residents of nursing homes. I remember the excitement and joy as these groups returned to share their experiences.

"I think she likes me!" confided a parishioner after her visit to someone in an assisted-living facility. This, for her, was a moment of grace and an extension of community.

I also think of graced moments during corporate worship. There were the multicolored silk streamers that descended from a church's ceiling during the Pentecost liturgy. There were the times I have renewed my baptismal vows when a new baby was brought into the Christian community. There are moments of silent reflection after readings when the church seems to hold its collective breath. And there are many occasions when I feel as if I am swept on a tide of voices, singing a beloved hymn.

Richard Foster believes that we are more likely to experience this kind of spiritual community if we are mindful of God during the week, as we go about our daily lives. As we cross streets and make beds and write at our desks, we can offer what we do to God—moment by moment. Then, when we gather for prayer in community, there is less of a disconnect between our workaday, individual mind-set and our corporate worship. We can also prepare ourselves for shared worship by taking extra time before a service to quiet our minds and open ourselves to God's presence.

Foster writes that "the Christian faith has strongly emphasized corporate worship. Even under highly dangerous circumstances, the early community was urged not to forsake the assembling of themselves together (Hebrews 10:25) and the Epistles speak frequently of the believers as 'the Body of Christ.'"[19]

In peril of their lives, the early Christians used symbols to point the way to secret gatherings, where the sacred rituals were celebrated and the sacred story was told. We, as the communion of saints, stand in that tradition as we worship freely and without fear.

This freedom of worship is a gift so easy to forget, but when I remember, I'm deeply grateful—grateful as Faith Matheny's epitaph describes in *Spoon River Anthology:*

> At first you will not know what they mean,
> And you may never know,
> And we may never tell you:

These sudden flashes in your soul,
Like lambent lightning on snowy clouds
At midnight when the moon is full.
They come in solitude, or perhaps
You sit with your friend, and all at once
A silence falls on speech....
You, two, have seen the secret together,
He sees it in you and you in him....
Be brave, all souls who have such visions!
As your body's alive as mine is dead,
You're catching a little whiff of the ether
Reserved for God Himself.[20]

*The heavens declare the glory of God; and the firmament sheweth
    his handywork.*
*Day unto day uttereth speech, and night unto night sheweth
    knowledge.*
There is no speech nor language, where their voice is not heard.
*Their line is gone out through all the earth, and their words to
    the end of the world. In them hath he set a tabernacle for
    the sun....*
*Let the words of my mouth, and the meditation of my heart,
    be acceptable in thy sight, O LORD, my strength, and my
    redeemer. (Psalm 19:1–4, 14)*

CURES FOR *Soulsickness* IN THE CITY

Stop: Read and Receive

1. Do you value having a spiritual community? What form does your spiritual community take in the city?

2. Which form of corporate worship appeals to you most? Do you need to change to a house of worship that's more congruent with your needs? A city offers so many different opportunities. Do you seek God's leading in finding the right spiritual home?

3. Have you had a bad experience with a spiritual community or faith tradition in the past? How did you react or respond to God about this? What's helped you overcome the painful or disturbing memory of that experience?

4. Where is "sacred space" for you? When you seek it in community, how does the relational aspect compare with the aesthetics of the place?

Yield: Reflect, Journal, or Discuss

5. Think about the times you reflect quietly with God. Do you notice any feelings of unworthiness about joining a spiritual community? What would you say to a trusted friend about this? Write down those thoughts in a letter to God right now. Put the letter in a place where you can pray over it for the next week. What are you noticing about your feelings of unworthiness?

6. For the next week, prayerfully ask God to lead you to the right *charisma* (Greek for "gift") for you to bring to your worship community.

7. Reflect today upon the ancient Hebrews and early Christians who worshiped in difficult circumstances—in the desert, in the catacombs, in Rome, in Greece. Write down or discuss with a friend what you're grateful to God for about your freedom to worship, even in the city, and as you feel led.

8. Ask yourself: How can I feel part of a unified body of individuals without a sense that I am losing my individuality? In what ways have I experienced the joy of being called to community and belonging? Write your thoughts, and revisit your answers over the next week, month, year.

Go: Experience and Engage

9. Identify the religious rituals that matter to you the most, and list them. For example, do you light candles as you ignite prayers? Do you say the Lord's Prayer as a practice? Do you attend a corporate worship assembly every certain day and time of the week? Keep this list in a way that you can continually add to it and perhaps mix things up from time to time in order to keep your faith exciting and ever deepening.

10. A friend has said that she will spend her retirement "filling myself up by giving myself away." Journal about ways you can do this too. Be as specific as you can about places and times to do this.

11. Identify a particular liturgical season that draws you most closely into community. Reflect with God on how you might bring others the Christmas spirit, for example, or the disciples' Pentecostal experience. Write down three ways and actually schedule these things on your calendar or in your day planner.

12. Today, think of yourself as one of God's people. Notice how this makes you feel. Offer thanks to God for bringing you into community.

FINDING GOD IN EMPTINESS
The Gateway to Worship

Holidays usually find us in familiar sanctuaries, but one Good Friday, I stopped into a small urban church, unknown to me before, to observe the Three Hours, that sacred time of reflection on Christ's Crucifixion.

I was late. There were a few people sitting quietly in the pews. A large crucifix was elevated before the altar. I walked up the aisle, my heels clicking loudly in the silence, and approached the altar. There was a hush all around me. It was almost three o'clock. Quietly, I drew near the cross to make a gesture of reverence.

Suddenly a burglar alarm sounded with such ferocity that I froze in shock. Never have I heard such an elaborate and loud alarm: sirens, bells, buzzers, and more, like an exaggerated car alarm on steroids.

Unwittingly, I'd set off the alarm by crossing an invisible electric eye around the altar. I don't know how long I stood there, frozen like the proverbial deer caught in the headlights, and I don't know how long I will go on recalling that terrible noise on the quietest, most somber day of the Christian year.

And so go the challenges of trying to find soul in the city. Even in a city's churches, there seem to be more situations that can isolate us or drain our spirits. But great experiences wait to be found too.

Thou Art Worthy

One amazing worship experience for me in the city was in a charismatic church. A thousand people surrounded me as we sang together in a plain, light-filled sanctuary, offering glory and honor and praise to God; I felt a surge of devotion as people raised their hands and lifted their voices.

Ever the introvert, I'd once assumed that I wouldn't feel comfortable with charismatic worship. I've since found myself drawn back to this church again and again. The "Prayer and Praise" evenings became important to me and have been added to my more traditional Sunday worship. I love the passion in the simple music and the powerful words glorifying God.

By contrast, I've also felt moved by much more formal worship in a beautiful city church, with glimmering stained glass and an intricately carved sanctuary. There, God's praise is sung by a highly polished men-and-boys choir, sometimes accompanied by hand bells. The choir's red robes shimmer in the dappled light; the worship style is much more ritualized.

I've also found deeply moving worship in an exquisite Jewish temple, a place that has been part of my spiritual journey. This temple is a magnificent, hushed, sacred space, where great stained-glass windows spill colors over the pews and draw your eyes upward. It is impossible to be here without sensing the glory of God and the power of time-honored faith. The service is rich, beautiful, and warm. Its liturgy differs in some ways from those practiced by the biblical communities, and it reflects a more contemporary sensibility. This temple also differs in some ways from Orthodox synagogues, where the setting may be more traditional, and the worship, in Hebrew, has changed little for thousands of years. But both enrich the sense that *God is present, God is among us.*

Another enriching experience has been found for a hundred and fifty years at a particular faithful, urban African American congregation. A longtime member there was a friend of mine, an assistant director of a homeless women's shelter, who traveled on a subway and two buses to get there. Her worship combined Bible study with call-and-response hymnody and a comprehensive sermon. After working hard all week, she filled her Sundays with worship, not as a duty, but as a joy. She would have certainly agreed with Paul in 1 Corinthians 10:31: "Whatsoever ye do, do all to the glory of God." Every act, for this devout woman, was for God's glory and so became worship.

Worship's Weave

What is typical city worship anyway?

"Is there such a thing?" Peter Hobson asks in *A Voice in the City.* "Some would deny it exists—surely as God is the same everywhere, so to worship him is the same wherever we go? God may be the same everywhere—but we are different. Wherever the cultures we live in differ, so also our worship of God must differ as well."[1]

A metropolitan area is unique in housing so many different forms of worship in one place. "City people, like people everywhere," Hobson continues, "are divided between evangelical and liberal, quiet and noisy, musical and tone-deaf—and so on."[2] Our different forms of worship ex-press this in a wondrous way. And just as we are distinguished by our differences, we are unified in our common search to find ways to worship the Holy One.

"God has offered us an incredible invitation to enter intimate relationship with himself," writes Gary W. Moon in his book *Falling for God.* "Relationship. Loving connection with the One who sketched the first atom, hung the stars without string, and crafted your soul.... Romantic? Yes. God's desire for love is stronger than your own."[3] And returning that love is an act of worship, right in the midst of a complex city.

But What Is Worship?

The actual word for *worship* comes from the Latin for "worthiness" or "ascribing worthiness."[4] God alone is worthy of our complete adoration and self-gift, but that definition may not take us far enough.

The apostle Paul proposes the following definition of true worship in Romans 12:1: "Present your bodies a living sacrifice, holy, acceptable unto God, which is your reasonable service."

Worship, then, is far more than ritual, style, or spiritual exercise. It's a transformational attitude, a way of life, a mind-set, and the heart's orientation, all of which undergirds personal and corporate prayer. Perhaps one could say that worship is enacted love.

In the words of Jesus (and the Hebrew prophets), "Thou shalt love the Lord thy God with all thy heart, and with all thy soul, and with all thy mind, and with all thy strength: this is the first commandment" (Mark 12:30).

This is our calling, wherever we are. And that includes the subway, the crosstown bus, the freeway and highway and byway.

"To worship is to experience Reality, to touch Life," Richard Foster says. "Worship is our response to the overtures of love from the heart of the Father.... It is kindled within us only when the Spirit of God touches our human spirit. Forms and rituals do not produce worship, nor does the disuse of forms and rituals.... We have not worshiped the Lord until Spirit touches spirit."[5]

So it was for John Wesley in the busy city of London on the evening of May 24, 1738. At a mission on Aldersgate Street, he listened to someone reading Martin Luther's "Preface to the Epistle to the Romans," and Wesley felt his heart "strangely warmed." He experienced anew God's great love, and from then on his ministry was changed. He became a dynamic preacher, "imparting to those who heard him the perception that Christianity was not so much a religion of laws and doctrines, but of love." He traveled far and wide on his preaching missions. "The whole world," he would say, "is my parish."[6]

Indeed, worship can happen anywhere and can take a powerful form. I remember feeling a strong sense of worship in a Paris hotel room. I was sixteen. This was my first trip to this beautiful city. Below my open window I could hear a street singer, smell garlic and strong coffee. I felt the presence of this new metropolis waiting for me. I was overwhelmed with a sense of gratitude to God, and I tossed far too many coins out the window at the stunned but grateful singer.

Richard Foster quotes a traditional hymn that captures how I felt: "Set my spirit free that I may worship Thee." These words are the basis of worship, he says. "Until God touches and frees our spirit, we cannot enter this realm. Singing, praying, praising all may lead us to worship, but worship is more than any of them."[7]

Whom Do We Worship?

To some observers a large urban center resembles a sterile desert or a baffling wilderness: a vast expanse of lifeless concrete and steel, where verdant earth is invisible and the sounds of nature itself seem far away. And sometimes, we may feel that the absence of nature (except for parks) means the absence of God.

On days when the cityscape seems like a concrete desert to me, I remind myself that God came to His people in the desert itself: "And I will dwell among the children of Israel, and will be their God. And they shall know that I am the LORD their God, that brought them forth out of the land of Egypt, that I may dwell among them: I am the LORD their God" (Exodus 29:45–46).

We can experience the Shekinah of God, the "immediate presence of God dwelling in the midst of his people," as Foster writes.[8]

I experienced this the time I sat next to a woman in the last pew of a large Protestant church. She wasn't singing, and she wore a blue plastic raincoat that squeaked when she moved. Three full shopping bags were at her feet, and her head was bowed in prayer. Throughout the service, she kept a worshipful silence or whispered words of worship. When the collection plate was passed, she reached into her pocket and produced a nickel—one single nickel—and placed it in the shining silver basin that contained a pile of checks and large bills.

Watching her, I thought of Jesus's story of the widow's mite: the poor woman who gave what little she had as an offering to God (see Mark 12:42–44).

"Worship is at once about who we are, about who or what our God is and about how we choose to live," Harold M. Best writes in *Unceasing Worship*. "It is about something that is quite simple but wrapped in mystery. It is about God himself, who has but one face.... It is about a world in which worship takes on a thousand faces."[9]

In a city, with its great diversity, this is especially true. "One free Sunday," writes Ray Bakke, "I visited twenty-two churches in different neighborhoods to celebrate what God was doing and how he was worshiped in the city. In 1966, I felt overpowered by the city and I asked God to enable me to love it. That revolutionized me."[10]

Jesus makes very clear, for all hearers and for all centuries, whom we are to worship: "Thou shalt worship the Lord thy God, and him only shalt thou serve" (Matthew 4:10). The Ten Commandments, as received by Moses, make a decisive order that rings throughout generations: "Thou shalt have no other gods before me" (Exodus 20:3).

"God is a Spirit," Jesus tells the Samaritan woman at the well (John 4:24), "and they that worship him must worship him in spirit and in truth."

The point is, we do not worship some localized deity who resides in a grove or grotto or stream. God, Lord of all, is everywhere. "For in him," writes Paul, "we live, and move, and have our being" (Acts 17:28). The Holy is not somehow more intensely present in nature, in pastoral or peaceful settings, although we may be conditioned to feel that this is so. The Holy is with us everywhere, in the crowds, the concrete—the city.

The Hebrews and early Christians were awed by this amazing, unmerited act—God had chosen to dwell among us. Surely, this was and is a call to worship. The infant church knew this, and believers worshiped in cities, such as Antioch, or deep below the ground in the catacombs of

Rome. A burial site might not be our choice for worship, but those courageous worshipers even brought beauty, sung and painted, to their torch-lit worship where the sun never shone. I think of them when the city can be distracting from the real meaning of worship. We can learn to tune out noise and distractions, but it's important not to tune out God.

It helps me to bring to mind the image of urban worship in an unlikely place: a booth at the parking exit of an urban mall. I'd stopped my car to pay my parking fee, but the booth seemed empty. I waited. No one, nothing. Finally, I got out of the car and peered into the booth.

The attendant was on his knees, lost in prayer.

"If God's reality is displayed to us in his Word or his world," John Piper writes in *Desiring God,* "and we do not then feel in our heart any grief or longing or hope or fear or awe or joy or confidence, then we may dutifully sing and pray and recite and gesture as much as we like, but it will not be real worship. We cannot honor God if our hearts are far from Him."[11]

In cities, whether I see them as desert or dreamscape, I can bring my heart to God in worship, private and corporate, and when I do, I join with all urban pray-ers in all their urban diversity. "The story of salvation begins in a garden (Genesis 1) and ends in a city (Revelation 22)," Ray Bakke writes in *The Urban Christian.* "The purpose of God is not to return to the garden, but to go on to the restored city."[12]

How Many Times?

Several years ago, a child asked me in a Sunday school class, "How many times does it happen?" I remember that small puzzled face, tilted toward mine. "Talking to God. Once a week?"

I think I told the child that we can talk to God as many times as we like—"it" doesn't "have" to happen only once a week. The child stared up at me, pondering my poor words.

"And can I talk to Jesus every day?"

"As often as you want," I said.

"And He always hears me?"

I nodded, realizing that I was reaffirming these fundamentals of worship for myself too.

"Worship is the continuous outpouring of all that I am, all that I do and all that I can ever become," Harold Best has said. God chooses us, and worship is our answer. "Outpouring surpasses measuring or filling quotas, even to the extent that it does not matter if some spills over." After all, he observes, "God is the uniquely Continuous Outpourer."[13]

I think of the woman in the gospels who expressed her worship by pouring out costly and fragrant ointment over the feet of Jesus, shortly before His crucifixion. She gave of herself, as we are called to give of ourselves, to God, and Best notes, with a certain irony, that "the room would not have been filled with such abundant fragrance had [the woman] merely tithed it out."[14]

How many of us have wished to have been the one to pour that fragrant, extravagant, beautiful ointment out for Jesus? How many of us have longed to participate in it, to also pour out ourselves to God?

We may wait for the perfect place, the perfect moment, but that's not what God expects. We don't have to be in our "Sunday best."

Richard J. Mouw worships God in fast-food restaurants. In his book *Praying at Burger King,* he tells how he continues a practice he learned as a child. He doesn't often find himself in "a praying mood while sitting in a restaurant," he says.[15] But then he doesn't pray *only* when he's feeling especially spiritual. "My restaurant prayers," Mouw writes, "are opportunities for me to pause and remind myself that there is indeed a God whose mercy reaches to me even when I am sitting in a fast-food booth with noisy kids running past me. I don't need to be in any kind of special mood to give myself that kind of reminder."[16]

Worship happens anywhere. "There is no place in all creation that is outside the scope of God's mercies—not even a Burger King," Mouw says. "Cheeseburgers and French fries are, properly understood, gifts from the Lord. The children running past are fashioned in the image of their creator. Fast-food restaurants are part of a larger world in which many are starving. I find it good for my soul to acknowledge these facts."[17]

Urban Sacred Space

"Places are sacred," Ray Bakke writes in *The Urban Christian*.[18]

Scripture shows this again and again. In Genesis 28:12, Jacob dreamed of a ladder connecting heaven and earth. Angels moved up and down the ladder. In his dream he had a holy encounter and afterward considered the place where this happened to be sacred space; and so he called the area Bethel (verse 19), meaning, "house of God."

Mount Sinai, where Moses received the Ten Commandments, is another sacred space, hallowed by God's presence and marked as holy by three faiths: Judaism, Christianity, and Islam.

In the gospels, Jesus, as boy and man, goes to the holy temple of Jerusalem (John 2) and to the sacred pool of Siloam (John 9). In the scene of the Transfiguration (Matthew 17), another mountaintop is transformed as Christ's true nature as God and man shines through.

"We can look at any place in London or Chicago as sacred because God is present and at work there," Bakke writes. "God sees that cities have personalities and assets. For the urban Christian and pastor there can be no throwaway real estate because 'the earth is the Lord's and everything in it' (Psalm 24:1), and that includes every neighborhood. Cities are a proper focus for redeeming ministry because they are treated in the Bible as persons and families and extensions of the people who live in them."[19]

Many urban spiritual communities use their sacred space to nurture the spirit in a variety of ways, often through a wide range of music: the universal language. I'm impressed with a city church that uses its space quite creatively: its pews, on certain occasions, are moved out of the way so that a labyrinth can be put down on the church floor. (Walking a labyrinth is an ancient form of meditation and reminds us of our spiritual journey.)

On the great vigil of Easter, at this urban church, the new fire of the Resurrection is kindled on a concrete plaza outside the sanctuary—and nestled against the skyscraper housing a branch of a worldwide financial institution.

Once the congregation returns to the church, this holy night's readings are done from various locations: the baptismal pool, the wall that holds the columbarium, and the lectern. Whether we prefer traditional or charismatic or emergent expressions of worship, the city creates sacred space for us all.

"We can all be timid Christians," Bakke reminds us, "when faced with modern urban conditions: the flight to the desert cave may have been more appealing [to the early Christians] than Constantine's city Christianity, just as the lonely commuter trapped in his car may feel more secure than he would feel walking home through a slum to a city address. But it is only by living in a city, with a theological vision for the city, that we can attempt to reach the city's people."[20] And provide spiritual support, I would add, for one another.

Ultimately, what makes space sacred is God in union with people. Spiritual communities are themselves a kind of invisible space, an area comprised of individuals knit together by worship and fellowship.

"For where two or three are gathered together in my name, there am I in the midst of them," Jesus promises (Matthew 18:20).

And there, worship happens.

Adoration as Worship

I often tend to think of worship as extroverted: singing, speaking, praying aloud. But there's a great power in silent worship as well. In many churches, pauses are left for reflection after readings and intercessions. I appreciate those times. I also cherish quiet times of worship in the back of the bus.

"When our reply to God is most direct of all, it is called *adoration*," Richard Foster writes in *Prayer: Finding the Heart's True Home*, "the spontaneous yearning of the heart to worship, honor, magnify, and bless God."[21]

Sometimes the prayer of adoration is a quiet, loving gaze. At other times, adoration is expressed in praise and thanksgiving. In either case, this kind of prayer always goes back to love: when we feel an outpouring of love, we cherish the beloved just for being.

C. S. Lewis cautions that we can get so caught up in life's business that we can forget God is always calling to us. One of the most common blocks to adoration, or the worship of God, is our own self-absorption, our conceit.[22]

However, for Lewis, the pleasures of worship, the adoration of God, make the blocks worth overcoming. Lewis refers to these pleasures as "shafts of glory." In such a state, prayer and worship pour out of us, he says, waking and sleeping. "To experience the tiny theophany [or manifestation of God's presence] is itself to adore."[23]

Our worship and adoration doesn't have to be a grand gesture. We may be disappointed if we wait to be swept off our feet with overwhelming worship right away. On some level, we may even fear this. But if we start small—as C. S. Lewis puts it, with "adoration in infinitesimals," a moment here, a moment there—our worship grows and glows and deepens.[24]

Worship Wherever

"In cities," a friend wrote, "I guess you worship wherever."

I guess so. There are an astonishing array of urban "wherevers" to focus on God and offer oneself, as Paul urged (Romans 12:1). There's also an astonishing witness to worship, noticeable once we begin to look around: the Orthodox Jewish pedestrian who is listening to prayers on his earphones; the Latino woman quietly saying her rosary as she waits on line at the city center urban post office; the taxi driver singing Gospel music along with a program on his radio; the homeless man, face raised to the sky, who calls, "Thank you, thank you," long after a donor has passed by.

Sometimes, a metropolis seems to hum with worship. Perhaps this is nothing to wonder at—the church itself came to be in a city; the New Jerusalem began as people gathered for worship in Christ's name. This occurred on the Feast of Pentecost when the Holy Spirit descended upon a group of urban Jewish Christians and inspired them; it was then that representatives of various nations miraculously heard the prayers in their own languages. Faith and worship, as we know, were spread throughout the cities of Asia Minor by the seemingly tireless apostle Paul, who visited large cities, including Ephesus and Corinth. The great apostle seemed to feel drawn, in my friend's words, to encourage worship "wherever."

What if we were to worship in such a personal way, finding such everyday, personal, even private venues conducive to prayer?

Climb Every Staircase

In small urban neighborhoods, my father told me that he'd seen people worshiping God on freight elevators, on fire escapes, and in hospital stairwells. In fact, the summer I spent as a chaplain intern, I was privileged to witness someone at prayer in an urban hospital's stairwell.

I was going so fast, unwilling to wait for the elevator, that I might have brushed past this woman at worship under an Exit sign.

"Are you okay?" I asked, as I mentally screeched to a halt.

"Oh yes. God's good."

I resumed my climb at a slower pace, and I've since recalled this reminder to slow down.

"Morning after morning," Rick Hamlin writes in his book *Finding God on the A Train,* "I come to this place in a world of distractions and I pray. I don't clock myself, but I use the subway stops as markers, guiding me in my ritual. I read from the 181st Street station to the 125th Street station, usually from the Bible," continues Hamlin, a magazine editor. "Then, at 125th Street I close my eyes. It's the express train, no more stops from there to 59th Street. At least five minutes of uninterrupted time. This is my time for God.... This early morning time of prayer feels like the most important. Without it, my day would fall apart, and I would forget whose I am."[25]

From fire escapes to stairwells to subways, urban worship happens. Most cities have fountains, and I've noticed people praying near them: in Rome, in Paris, and across America. I don't mean the wish you might make as you toss a coin in Rome's famous Trevi Fountain. I mean real prayer.

I gravitate toward water myself, and I often meet other people there seeking a little soul in the city. There are senior people who pray as they feed the birds in urban piazzas, and senior executives who sit quietly, listening to the splash of water and reading the Bible. In many cities there are tiny parks—"vest-pocket parks," as they're called—where there's often a waterfall. I once saw a young couple hold hands and kneel down to pray together before the cascade of water down a steep, sleek city wall.

Another gathering place for soul seekers are cafés. I love the seasons when restaurants open their french doors or storefronts and people sit looking out at the street—or on it. Sidewalk cafés are an urban delight, and if you sit in one for a while, you'll notice there are often people who linger—sometimes drinking coffee and watching the passersby, sometimes sketching or writing. And sometimes, I see a pocket Bible in someone's hands, a cross or rosary or flower turned around and around, in silent, reverent contemplation.

Come Up Higher

I always feel worshipful in a city when I'm on a building's high floor. Perhaps this is simply a childlike sense that God is in the sky or a residue of that, but I'd prefer to think this feeling is some dim echo of biblical encounters with the Holy—like Moses on Sinai's peak and Jesus Christ transfigured on a mountain.

I especially think of God when I'm at the top of Manhattan's Rockefeller Center, where there's a tiered observation deck, offering a panoramic outdoor view of New York City from the sixty-seventh, sixty-ninth, and seventieth floors. From there, the view spreads in all its amazing detail, and I marvel at what God has created through human hands. Skyscrapers stand vigil around the open expanse of Central Park, bridges surface and arch all around, and the buses and the buildings take on new beauty.

I'm not alone in feeling worshipful high above urban space. Twenty years ago I wrote about a humble man who was a maintenance mechanic's assistant at the Statue of Liberty. I've never forgotten Charlie DeLeo's sense of worship. Every morning before work, DeLeo, a devoted Christian, would go up quietly to the statue's famous torch, where he would offer his prayers to God. He regarded this place as a shrine. DeLeo took some teasing from co-workers, but he only smiled and persisted in prayer. In his perch, high above the New York harbor and Manhattan skyline, he experienced God's presence and a desire to respond. I can't know what words he spoke, but it's enough for me to know that he spoke them. And I believe he had a strong sense of the many immigrants who flooded past his private "chapel."[26]

From on high, Charlie too must have felt awe, love, wonder, and gratitude. He too must have seen from his perch, high above a city, that God is everywhere—even, as the psalmist says, in the depths of the sea (Psalm 139:9–10). Whether from the Statue of Liberty, Sears Tower in Chicago, Space Needle in Seattle, or on the rim of the Grand Canyon, the height offers a new angle with which to view human life. The child in me whispers, *So this is how God the Father sees us....*

At night, from a high floor in a city, the lights seem to shimmer, and I think again of those millions of different lives behind each light. It's a thoroughly urban experience of worship, as if the city below is somehow mirroring the stars that God has set in their courses above us. It seems at times that the creation is shining back at its Creator; perhaps, in the end, that's what we do when we worship: we shine back a little of that light that is God's.

There always comes a point in adoration when the boundaries of language break down and there are no words to describe what we feel. In the holiest of moments, whether they're on a mountaintop or the Top of the Rock, we are speechless, except perhaps for a holy few, as Thornton Wilder's narrator suggests in his play *Our Town*: the poets and the saints.

I was speechless, I remember, looking down from the roof of Chartres Cathedral, where I gazed out at an eight-hundred-year-old town and realized that it was young and beautiful in God's sight. I'd climbed to that rooftop, eleven stories high, so that I could write about what I saw.

Instead, perched above that venerable city, I knew no words: only worship.

Rejoice in the LORD, O ye righteous: for praise is comely for the upright.

Praise the LORD with harp: sing unto him with the psaltery and an instrument of ten strings.

Sing unto him a new song; play skilfully with a loud noise.

For the word of the LORD is right; and all his works are done in truth.

He loveth righteousness and judgment: the earth is full of the goodness of the LORD. (Psalm 33:1–5)

CURES FOR *Soulsickness* IN THE CITY

Stop: Read and Receive

1. Do I embrace or enjoy or avoid worship? Is it a duty or a habit or something more?

2. In the context of the city where you live or spend time, what do you hope to find to deepen your experience in corporate worship? What hinders and what helps?

3. Are you seeking a deeper experience in your personal worship? And again, what hinders or helps in a city?

4. Have you ever let yourself go into a prayer time that's focused more on gratitude and love of God, without necessarily including petition?

Yield: Reflect, Journal, or Discuss

5. Do you ever secretly think that worship outside in nature is superior to worship in the city? If so, in what ways? If not, why?

6. Have you ever had an experience such as Charlie DeLeo's or something similar? Describe that time. Where were you physically? emotionally? spiritually? What happened— where and how and when? How has that changed you (from what, to what)?

7. Is there an aspect of ritual to your worship? What forms or rituals or practices help you open yourself to God's presence?

8. Journal on this or discuss with a friend: how does worship affect and enrich your life in the city? Identify at least two ways.

Go: Experience and Engage

9. Today, worship God in such a "mundane" place as the subway or a bus.

10. Today, use music as a part of your worship. Read a hymn or listen to a CD that lifts your spirit and becomes a sweet sound to God.

11. This month, experiment with contemplative silence as a form of worship.

FINDING GOD IN THE CONCRETE

The Gateway to Gratitude

There is a Celtic belief that in "thin places," the Holy is especially close, shining through the material world. The great medieval cathedrals are said to be built on such areas, as is Stonehenge and the Pyramids. To my surprise, I've come to affirm that cities, too, reveal those thin places.

For a long time, I'd thought that I would never feel that "thinness" away from such places as Chartres in France or the lakes in Maine. During my girlhood summers in Maine, near the Rangeley Lakes, I used to lie in my sleeping bag with the woods whispering around me. I would stare up, awestruck, at the numberless stars in the vast night sky arching above me. City child that I was, I felt especially lost, found, and blessed by those nights of gazing upward.

In his famous play *Long Day's Journey into Night,* Eugene O'Neill shared a similar experience:

For a moment I lost myself—actually lost my life. I was set free! I dissolved in the…high dim-starred sky! I belonged, without past or future, within peace and unity and a wild joy, within something greater than my own life…to Life itself! To God.… For a second, you see—and seeing the secret, [you] are the secret.[1]

Now at night, when I look out at the lights of a great city, I think of O'Neill's words: I see the secret; I am the secret. I cannot see the stars, but I can see the lights that signify life. Mine is one of them, one with them. Seen from the air, a city's lights glimmer as if they are connected. Seen from the street, the lights seem to stream upward. As I stand and gaze above me, I feel that I am a part of all the cities that ever were. I think of all those lives behind the countless lit windows that spread before me, those countless human stories shimmering together in the darkness. It seems miraculous to me now, how all those lights, and lives, can coexist together. This is one of the city's great strengths and gifts.

In cities one can see "the secret" so often, multiplied over and over— and be a part of it. "You fully accept the whole grain of this given universe, as you are fully one with the whole," writes David Steindl-Rast in his book *Gratefulness, the Heart of Prayer.* Your lit window joins the myriad of others in the cityscape's glimmering night. To live in a city is to live in a small galaxy where every point of light is joined to the others.[2]

I find myself thinking of thin places on the day-lit city streets as well. On the pavements, on the asphalt, on the avenues, scores of strangers have said, "Thank you," to me. Taxi drivers. Vendors. Pedestrians. A homeless couple. A blind woman. Delivery men. Doormen. Kids on roller skates. A construction worker. Most of these people responded only to a smile, a word, a gesture of making way for one another. And in each stranger, there is a glimpse of God.

Grit and Gratitude

In cities we must learn to surrender many things: large amounts of privacy, space, quiet, and leeway. If we aren't able to give up and give way, we won't survive. Last night, for example, I attended a sold-out concert in a packed hall, and I dined in an equally crowded café. And yet, over the din, everyone around me was polite, even merry, and grateful for great music, good food, and a glorious evening. There was a sense of connection between all those strangers and the One who brought us together.

The urban practice of surrender may help us surrender to God in prayer. This is perhaps one of the great challenges of spiritual life. Urban people learn surrender the moment they step onto the street. But what if, as C. S. Lewis writes, we each learned to surrender in our spiritual lives?

> The terrible thing, the almost impossible thing, is to hand over your whole self—all your wishes and precautions—to Christ.... It comes the very moment you wake up each morning. All your wishes and hopes for the day rush at you like wild animals. And the first job each morning consists simply in shoving them all back; in listening to that other voice, taking that other point of view, letting that other larger, stronger, quieter life come flowing in. And so on, all day.[3]

It's amazing to me that we all survive the innumerable perils of a busy city—and most of the time, in an orderly, careful way. "The greatest sacrament that survival administers is gratitude," writes Kelly Murphy Mason, who escaped from the World Trade Center on 9/11, rescued by an "angel in a business suit." In her article "The Sacrament of Gratitude," Mason expresses her renewed sense of the sacred in her city: New York. After a bike ride around a park, she writes:

> I ate a sacramental hot dog (the best I'd ever tasted) from a sacramental vendor working a sacramental cart at a sacramental entrance to the sacramental park that had been blocks away from me for years.... Never have I been so convinced of the sacredness

of participating in the commonplace, or the blessedness of drawing breath, or of the privilege of moving through this world day after day.[4]

Mason's experience, like that of all 9/11 survivors, is special. But I believe that her gratitude to God is possible for all who live and work in cities. Nowhere else are we so interdependent, so interconnected. Nowhere else have we so many faces in which to see the Holy One, in whose image we are made. Nowhere else have we so many opportunities to see Jesus Christ in the poor, and to feed, visit, and touch Him through them.

There is a special sense of gratitude in cities: for the bus that waits, the pedestrian who steps aside, the taxi that stops, the man who slows the revolving door, the woman's murmured, "Excuse me," and simply for surviving, as my homeless friends would say.

Yes, in the city there is grit. There is crime. There is garbage. And there is grace.

Soon after 9/11, Kelly Murphy Mason wrote that a barbeque grill caught fire in her neighborhood park, and when the firemen arrived, they were mobbed by strangers reaching out to touch them, strangers who kept chanting, over and over, "Thank you, thank you, thank you."[5]

These are words we say to God, in cities, as we think of the fires put out, the lights put on, the dozens of languages put together, all in one place.

So it was on the first Pentecost, when the gift of the Holy Spirit was given to people of every nation in a great city.

So it is today in cities around the world.

God is in the crowds, the sounds, the speed, the spiraling stone spaces, the "thin places" where, if we take time to look, we find the Holy One everywhere. And we say, *Thank You. Thank You. Thank You.*

*The heavens declare the glory of God; and the firmament sheweth
     his handywork.*
*Day unto day uttereth speech, and night unto night sheweth
     knowledge.*
There is no speech nor language, where their voice is not heard.
*Their line is gone out through all the earth, and their words to
     the end of the world. In them hath he set a tabernacle for the
     sun. (Psalm 19:1–4)*

CURES FOR *Soulsickness* IN THE CITY

Stop: Read and Receive

1. Which aspects of a city seems most graced to you?
2. Where in the city do you find the greatest obstacles to a sense of gratitude to God?
3. What urban moment in your day makes you feel a sense of thanks to God? In what ways? Why or how so?

Yield: Reflect, Journal, or Discuss

4. Compose a brief prayer of gratitude for the grace you feel in the town or city where you live or spend time.
5. Begin a running City Grace Journal and note the aspects of your town where you feel God's presence most strongly.
6. Continue a City Prayer Journal, noting places, situations, sights, and people who lead you to feel prayerful.
7. Notice the times you feel, as the playwright Eugene O'Neill described, that you are lost in God's presence—wherever you are in the city.
8. Journal about the connectedness you see in city lights at night.

Go: Experience and Engage

9. Make a list of cities especially on your mind and heart. Pray for them each day for the next two weeks, and pray too for people in all the cities of the world.
10. Find a special time of day when you feel urban grace and make a mental appointment with God to give thanks at that time.

11. Today, sit in a city café and say a prayer for everyone around you.
12. This month set aside time to write a letter to your city and include a blessing for its people.

NOTES

Chapter 1

1. Linthicum, *City of God*, back cover copy.
2. Moore, *Care of the Soul*, xix.
3. Wright, *Mother Teresa's Prescription*, 19.
4. Buechner, *Magnificent Defeat*, 18.
5. Buechner, *Hungering Dark*, 12–13.
6. Augustine, *Confessions*, 42.
7. Hopkins, *Poems and Prose*, 27.

Chapter 2

1. Horwitz, *Spiritual Activist*, 3.
2. Merton, *Conjectures*, 156.
3. Lewis, "Transfiguration of Moses."
4. Bill, *Mind the Light*, 70–72.
5. Bill, *Mind the Light*, 71.
6. Merton, *Conjectures*, 213.
7. Bill, *Mind the Light*, 71.
8. Day, "Room for Christ," 2.
9. Day, "Room for Christ," 2.
10. Foster, *Celebration of Discipline*, 96.
11. Bloom, *Beginning to Pray*, 55–56.
12. Bloom, *Beginning to Pray*, 49.
13. Bloom, *Beginning to Pray*, 55.

14. Kelly, *Testament of Devotion*, 12–13.
15. Kelly, *Testament of Devotion*, 15.
16. Kelly, *Testament of Devotion*, 9.
17. *Webster's Ninth New Collegiate Dictionary*, s.v. "crowd."
18. Teresa, *Everything Starts from Prayer*, 50.
19. Teresa, *Everything Starts from Prayer*, 48.
20. Teresa, *Everything Starts from Prayer*, 53.
21. Teresa, *Everything Starts from Prayer*, 26–29.
22. Teresa, *Everything Starts from Prayer*, 23.
23. Bill, *Mind the Light*, 76.

Chapter 3

1. Merton, *Conjectures*, 308.
2. Horwitz, *Spiritual Activist*, 27.
3. Teresa, *Everything Starts from Prayer*, 22.
4. Teresa, *Everything Starts from Prayer*, 22.
5. Yamanouchi in Birkel, *Silence and Witness*, 41.
6. Griffin, *Doors into Prayer*, 8.
7. Underhill, *The Spiritual Life*, 61.
8. Augustine, *Confessions*, 42.
9. Griffin, *Doors into Prayer*, 12.
10. Griffin, *Doors into Prayer*, 12.
11. Bloom, *Beginning to Pray*, 92–94.
12. Bloom, *Beginning to Pray*, 94.
13. Kelly, *Testament of Devotion*, 15.
14. Yancey, *Finding God*, 124.
15. Tozer, *Pursuit of God*, 56.
16. Merton, *Conjectures*, 178.
17. Bill, *Holy Silence*, 5.
18. Bill, *Holy Silence*, 37.
19. Moore, *Discovering Everyday Spirituality*.
20. Sutton in Bill, *Holy Silence*, 52.
21. Sutton in Bill, *Holy Silence*, 52–53.

Chapter 4

1. Gleick, *Faster,* 9, 13.
2. *You've Got Mail,* DVD.
3. Frost, *Poetry,* 22.
4. *Grand Canyon,* VHS.
5. Wordsworth, "Intimations of Immortality," Ode 536.
6. Buechner, *Hungering Dark,* 74.
7. Buechner, *Hungering Dark,* 74–75.
8. Laubach, "Opening Windows," 103.
9. Horwitz, *Spiritual Activist,* 13.
10. Griffin, *Doors into Prayer,* 53.
11. Rahner, *Encounters,* 45–52.
12. Rahner, *Encounters,* 45–52.
13. Griffin, *Doors into Prayer,* 43.
14. Griffin, *Doors into Prayer,* 6.
15. Warren, *Purpose-Driven Life,* 87.
16. Warren, *Purpose-Driven Life,* 74.
17. Julian in Chilson, *All Will Be Well,* 35.
18. Julian in Chilson, *All Will Be Well,* 126.
19. Pennington, *Centered Living,* 16, 55.
20. Matthews, *Making Room for God,* 25.
21. Pennington, *Centered Living,* p. xx.
22. Pascal, *Pensées,* 43.
23. Matthews, *Making Room for God,* 20.
24. Kelly, *Testament of Devotion,* 17.

Chapter 5

1. Jeon, *City Dharma,* 114.
2. Konigsberg, "New Class War."
3. Hamlin, *Finding God on the A Train,* 5.
4. Hybels, *Too Busy Not to Pray,* 1–2, 12.
5. Lewis, *Joyful Christian,* 186.
6. Masters, *Spoon River Anthology,* 314.

7. Levy, "(Some) Attention."

8. Benson, *Trappist,* VHS.

9. Lewis, *Joyful Christian,* 90.

10. Davis, *Time of Your Life,* 141.

11. Davis, *Time of Your Life,* 141.

12. Davis, *Time of Your Life,* 143.

13. Davis, *Time of Your Life,* 143.

14. Lawrence, *Practice of the Presence,* 12.

15. Lawrence, *Practice of the Presence,* 12.

16. "Good-bye to Frank Laubach, Apostle of Literacy," Christian History Institute, June 11, 1970, http://chi.gospelcom.net/DAILYF/2002/06/daily-06-11-2002.shtml.

17. Disrud, "Sabbath Time."

18. Edwards, *Sabbath Time,* 67.

19. Edwards, *Sabbath Time,* 67.

20. Parker in Disrud, "Sabbath Time."

21. Disrud, "Sabbath Time."

22. Baab, *Sabbath Keeping,* 10.

23. Baab, *Sabbath Keeping,* 10.

24. Muller, *Sabbath,* 1.

25. Muller, *Sabbath,* 1.

26. "Good-bye to Frank Laubach," http://chi.gospelcom.net.

Chapter 6

1. Foster, *Celebration of Discipline,* 86.

2. Willard, *Renovation of the Heart,* 87.

3. Tozer, *Pursuit of God,* 111–13.

4. Tozer, *Pursuit of God,* 110.

5. Heidish, *Woman Called Moses,* 125–29.

6. Moon, *Falling for God,* 108.

7. Yount, *Spiritual Simplicity,* 36.

8. Foster, *Celebration of Discipline,* 84.

9. Foster, *Celebration of Discipline,* 84.

10. Hammarskjold, *Markings,* 90.

11. Hammarskjold, *Markings,* 91.

12. Hammarskjold, *Markings,* 93.

13. Pierce, *Choosing Simplicity,* 25.

14. Foster, *Celebration of Discipline,* 88.

15. Yount, *Spiritual Simplicity,* 109.

16. Yount, *Spiritual Simplicity,* 108.

17. Yount, *Spiritual Simplicity,* 109.

18. Rosenwald, "Steak-Filled Room."

19. Kelly, *Testament of Devotion,* 3.

Chapter 7

1. Wilder, *Our Town,* 88.

2. Wilder, *Our Town,* 107.

3. Kristeller, "Power of the Creative Arts," www.mindspirit.org.

4. Best, *Unceasing Worship,* 21.

5. Beckett, "Sister Wendy."

6. Norris, *Cloister Walk,* 151–52.

7. Dickinson, *Selected Poems,* 121.

8. Dickinson, *Selected Poems,* 169–70.

9. Hamma, *Landscapes of the Soul,* 14, 17.

10. Merton, *Conjectures,* 177.

11. Bergman, *Spiritual Traveler,* 235.

12. Heidish, "Queen of Chartres," 80.

13. Carmelite Newsletter, Christmas 2006.

14. Teresa of Avila, *Interior Castle.*

15. Matthews, *Making Room for God,* 5.

Chapter 8

1. Gould, *Deliberate Acts of Kindness,* 2, 4–5.

2. Gould, *Deliberate Acts of Kindness,* 5–6.

3. Rolheiser, *Holy Longing,* 65.

4. Warren, *Purpose-Driven Life,* 257.

5. Davis, *Time of Your Life,* 171.

6. Rolheiser, *Holy Longing,* 73.

7. Foster, *Celebration of Discipline,* 126.

8. Foster, *Prayer,* 191.

9. Foster, *Prayer,* 191–92.

10. Bloom, *Beginning to Pray,* 112–13.

11. Teresa, *Everything Starts from Prayer,* 117.

12. Teresa, *Everything Starts from Prayer,* 118.

13. Ellsberg, *All Saints,* 324.

14. Ellsberg, *All Saints,* 324–25.

15. Goulart, *One Good Work,* 9.

16. Goulart, *One Good Work,* 9–11.

Chapter 9

1. Cited in Jeon, *City Dharma,* 12.

2. Spurgeon, *All of Grace,* 7.

3. Holtz, *Downtown Monks,* 14.

4. Rolheiser, *Holy Longing,* 67.

5. Dickens, *Christmas Carol.*

6. Laubach, "Opening Windows," 104.

7. Jeon, *City Dharma,* 131–32.

8. Rolheiser, *Holy Longing,* 67.

9. Pennington, *Centered Living,* 93.

10. Pennington, *Centered Living,* 21.

11. *Webster's Ninth New Collegiate Dictionary,* s.v. "mercy."

12. *Amazing Grace* with Bill Moyers, VHS.

13. Waldron, *Poetry as Prayer,* 28–40.

14. Waldron, *Poetry as Prayer,* 28–40.

15. Waldron, *Poetry as Prayer,* 34.

16. Waldron, *Poetry as Prayer,* 56.

17. Waldron, *Poetry as Prayer,* 64.

Chapter 10

1. Spong, "The Urban Church," 828.

2. PBS, "Storefront Churches," www.pbs.org.

3. PBS, "Storefront Churches," www.pbs.org.

4. PBS, "Storefront Churches," www.pbs.org.

5. Gonzalez, "Church's Challenge."

6. Spong, "The Urban Church," 828.

7. Bakke, *Urban Christian,* 152.

8. Bakke, *Urban Christian,* 152.

9. Bakke, *Theology,* 63.

10. Bakke, *Theology,* 63.

11. Kostarelos, *Feeling the Spirit,* 4.

12. Orsi, *Gods of the City,* 232–33.

13. Orsi, *Gods of the City,* 292.

14. Ellsberg, *All Saints,* 317.

15. Willard, *Renovation,* 87.

16. Warren, *Purpose-Driven Life,* 145.

17. Warren, *Purpose-Driven Life,* 142.

18. Warren, *Purpose-Driven Life,* 138.

19. Foster, *Celebration of Discipline,* 163–64.

20. Masters, *Spoon River Anthology,* 310.

Chapter 11

1. Hobson, *Voice in the City,* 15.

2. Hobson, *Voice in the City,* 15.

3. Moon, *Falling for God,* 3.

4. *Webster's Ninth New Collegiate Dictionary,* s.v. "worship."

5. Foster, *Celebration of Discipline,* 158.

6. Ellsberg, *All Saints,* 263–64.

7. Foster, *Celebration of Discipline,* 159.

8. Foster, *Celebration of Discipline,* 158.

9. Best, *Unceasing Worship,* 17.

10. Bakke, *Urban Christian,* 63.

11. Piper, *Desiring God,* 32.

12. Bakke, *Urban Christian,* 78.

13. Best, *Unceasing Worship,* 21.

14. Best, *Unceasing Worship,* 20.

15. Mouw, *Praying at Burger King,* 3–4.

16. Mouw, *Praying at Burger King,* 4.

17. Mouw, *Praying at Burger King,* 5.

18. Bakke, *Urban Christian,* 62.

19. Bakke, *Urban Christian,* 63.

20. Bakke, *Urban Christian,* 85.

21. Foster, *Prayer,* 81.

22. Cited in Foster, *Prayer,* 87.

23. Lewis in Foster, *Prayer,* 88.

24. Foster, *Prayer,* 90.

25. Hamlin, *Finding God on the A Train,* 4–5.

26. Heidish, "Lady of the Island," 66–71.

Chapter 12

1. O'Neill, *Long Day's Journey,* 153.

2. Steindl-Rast, *Gratefulness,* 23.

3. Lewis, *Mere Christianity,* 168–69.

4. Mason, "Sacrament of Gratitude."

5. Mason, "Sacrament of Gratitude."

BIBLIOGRAPHY

Amazing Grace with Bill Moyers. VHS. Beverly Hills: PBS Home Video, 1990.

Augustine. *The Confessions.* Translated by Maria Boulding. Hyde Park, NY: New City, 1997.

Baab, Lynne M. *Sabbath Keeping: Finding Freedom in the Rhythms of Rest.* Downers Grove, IL: InterVarsity, 2005.

Bakke, Ray. *A Theology as Big as the City.* Downers Grove, IL: InterVarsity, 1997.

———. *The Urban Christian: Effective Ministry in Today's Urban World.* Downers Grove, IL: InterVarsity, 1987.

Basden, Paul A., ed. *Exploring the Worship Spectrum: Six Views.* Grand Rapids: Zondervan, 2004.

Beckett, Sister Wendy. "Sister Wendy in Conversation with Bill Moyers." VHS. Boston: WGBH Educational Foundation, 1977.

Benson, Herbert. *Trappist.* VHS. Directed by Robert G. Maier. Charlotte, NC: Paulist Media Works, 1997.

Bergman, Edward F. *The Spiritual Traveler: New York City: The Guide to Spiritual Spaces and Peaceful Places.* Mahwah, NJ: HiddenSpring, 2001.

Best, Harold M. *Unceasing Worship: Biblical Perspectives on Worship and the Arts.* Downers Grove, IL: InterVarsity, 2003.

Bill, J. Brent. *Holy Silence: The Gift of Quaker Spirituality.* Brewster, MA: Paraclete, 2005.

———. *Mind the Light: Learning to See with Spiritual Eyes.* Brewster, MA: Paraclete, 2006.

Birkel, Michael L. *Silence and Witness: The Quaker Tradition.* Marynoll, NY: Orbis, 2004.

Bishop, Jim. *The Day Christ Died.* New York: Harper Brothers, 1957.

Bloom, Anthony. *Beginning to Pray.* Mahwah, NJ: Paulist, 1970.

Buechner, Frederick. *The Hungering Dark.* New York: HarperSanFrancisco, 1969.

———. *The Magnificent Defeat.* New York: HarperSanFrancisco, 1966.

Carmelite Monastery. Christmas 2006 Newsletter. Carmel, CA: Carmelite Monastery, 2006.

Carson, D. A., ed. *Worship by the Book.* Grand Rapids, MI: Zondervan, 2002.

Chilson, Richard. *All Will Be Well: Based on the Classic Spirituality of Julian of Norwich.* Notre Dame, IN: Ave Maria, 1995.

Christian History Institute. "Good-bye to Frank Laubach, Apostle of Literacy." June 11, 1970. http://chi.gospelcom.net/DAILYF/2002/06/daily-06-11-2002.shtml.

Conn, Harvie M., and Manuel Ortiz. *Urban Ministry: The Kingdom, the City, and the People of God.* Downers Grove, IL: InterVarsity, 2001.

Davis, Susie. *The Time of Your Life: Finding God's Rest in Your Busy Schedule.* Wheaton, IL: Crossway, 2006.

Day, Dorothy. "Room for Christ." *The Catholic Worker,* December 1945.

Dickens, Charles. *A Christmas Carol.* New York: Puffin Books, 2001.

Dickinson, Emily. *Selected Poems of Emily Dickinson.* New York: Random House, 1924.

Disrud, Thomas. "Sabbath Time." Sermon, First Unitarian Church of Portland, October 23, 2005.

Dosick, Wayne. *Living Judaism: The Complete Guide to Jewish Belief, Tradition, and Practice.* New York: HarperCollins, 1995.

Duquoc, Christian, ed. *Spirituality in the Secular City.* Mahwah, NJ: Paulist, 1966.

Edwards, Tilden. *Living Simply Through the Day: Spiritual Survival in a Complex Age.* Mahwah, NJ: Paulist, 1998.

———. *Sabbath Time: Understanding and Practice for Contemporary Christians.* Minneapolis: Seabury, 1982.

Ellsberg, Robert. *All Saints: Daily Reflections on Saints, Prophets, and Witnesses for Our Time.* New York: Crossroad, 1997.

Elmore, Michael F. *Stress and Spirituality: Conquering the Stress of Life and Achieving Your Spiritual Potential.* Plymouth, MA: MCK, 2002.

Falk, Marcia, *The Book of Blessings: A New Prayerbook for the Weekdays, the Sabbath and New Moon.* New York: HarperCollins, 1996.

Foster, Richard J. *Celebration of Discipline: The Path to Spiritual Growth.* New York: HarperSanFrancisco, 1978.

———. *Freedom of Simplicity: Finding Harmony in a Complex World.* New York: Harper Paperbacks, 1981.

———. *Prayer: Finding the Heart's True Home.* New York: HarperCollins, 1992.

———, and James Bryan Smith, eds. *Devotional Classics: Selected Readings for Individuals and Groups.* New York: HarperSanFrancisco, 1990, 2005.

Frost, Robert. *The Poetry of Robert Frost.* Edited by Edward Connery Lathem. New York: Holt, Rinehart, and Winston, 1969.

Gleick, James. *Faster: The Acceleration of Just About Everything.* New York: Random House, 1999.

Godden, Rumer. *In This House of Brede.* New York: Viking, 1969.

Goetz, Dave. *Death by Suburb: How to Keep the Suburbs from Killing Your Soul.* New York: HarperCollins, 2006.

Gonzalez, David. "A Church's Challenge: Holding On to Its Young." *New York Times,* January 16, 2007.

Goulart, Frances Sheridan. *One Good Work at a Time: Simple Things You Can Do to Make a Difference.* Notre Dame, IN: Sorin, 2006.

Gould, Meredith. *Deliberate Acts of Kindness: Service as a Spiritual Practice.* New York: Image, 2002.

Grand Canyon. VHS. Directed by Lawrence Kasdan. Los Angeles: Twentieth Century Fox, 1992.

Griffin, Emilie. *Clinging: The Experience of Prayer.* New York: Harper and Row, 1984.

———. *Doors into Prayer: An Invitation.* Brewster, MA: Paraclete, 2005.

———. *Wilderness Time: A Guide for Spiritual Retreat.* San Francisco: HarperSanFrancisco, 1997.

———. *Wonderful and Dark Is This Road: Discovering the Mystic Path.* Brewster, MA: Paraclete, 2004.

Hamlin, Rick. *Finding God on the A Train: A Journey into Prayer.* New York: HarperCollins, 1997.

Hamma, Robert M. *Landscapes of the Soul: A Spirituality of Place.* Notre Dame, IN: Ave Maria, 1999.

Hammarskjold, Dag. *Markings.* New York: Ballantine Books, 1983.

Harper, Nile. *Urban Churches: Vital Signs: Beyond Charity Toward Justice.* Grand Rapids: Eerdmans, 1999.

Heidish, Marcy. "Lady of the Island." *Hemispheres,* July 1998.

———. "Queen of Chartres." *Hemispheres,* October 1997.

———. *Who Cares? Simple Ways to Reach Out.* Notre Dame, IN: Ave Maria, 1996.

———. *A Woman Called Moses.* New York: Bantam, 1978.

Hobson, Peter. *A Voice in the City: Worship for Urban People.* London: Scripture Union, 1993.

Holtz, Albert. *Downtown Monks: Sketches of God in the City.* Notre Dame, IN: Ave Maria, 2000.

Hopkins, Gerard Manley. *Poems and Prose.* Edited by W. H. Garner. New York: Penguin, 1963.

Horwitz, Claudia. *The Spiritual Activist: Practices to Transform Your Life, Your Work, and Your World.* New York: Penguin, 2002.

Hybels, Bill. *Too Busy Not to Pray: Slowing Down to Be with God.* Downers Grove, IL: InterVarsity, 1998.

Jeon, Arthur. *City Dharma: Keeping Your Cool in the Chaos.* New York: Three Rivers, 2004.

Kelly, Thomas R. *A Testament of Devotion.* New York: Harper & Brothers, 1941. Reprinted with introduction, New York: HarperCollins, 1992. Page references are to the 1992 edition.

Konigsberg, Eric. "A New Class War: The Haves vs. the Have Mores." *New York Times,* November 19, 2006.

Kostarelos, Frances. *Feeling the Spirit: Faith and Hope in an Evangelical Black Storefront Church.* Columbia: University of South Carolina, 1995.

Kristeller, Julia. "The Power of the Creative Arts in Psychotherapy and Spirituality." Psychotherapy and Spirituality Institute. www.mindspirit.org/creativearts.htm.

Laubach, Frank. *Living Words: Compiled from the Writings of Frank C. Laubach.* Grand Rapids: Zondervan, 1967.

———. "Opening Windows to God." In *Devotional Classics: Selected Readings for Individuals and Groups.* Edited by Richard J. Foster and James Bryan Smith. New York: HarperCollins, 1989.

Lawrence, Brother. *The Practice of the Presence of God.* New Kensington, PA: Whitaker House, 1982.

Levy, Steven. "(Some) Attention Must Be Paid." *Newsweek,* March 27, 2006.

Lewis, C. S. *The Joyful Christian.* New York: Macmillan, 1977.

———. *Mere Christianity.* New York: Macmillan, 1952.

Lewis, Mark. "The Transfiguration of Moses, of Jesus…and of You! Reflections on the Lessons for the Feast of the Transfiguration." Sermon, Church of Our Savior, Secaucus, NJ, August 6, 2000.

Linthicum, Robert C. *City of God, City of Satan: A Biblical Theology of the Urban Church.* Grand Rapids: Zondervan, 1991.

Luther, Martin. *Martin Luther: Selections from His Writing.* Edited by John Dillenberger. New York: Anchor, Doubleday, 1958.

Mason, Kelly Murphy. "The Sacrament of Gratitude." Beliefnet, 2001. www.beliefnet.com/story/89/story_8926_1.html.

Masters, Edgar Lee. *Spoon River Anthology: An Annotated Edition.* Edited by John E. Hallwas. Urbana: University of Illinois, 1992.

Matthews, Melvyn. *Making Room for God: A Guide to Contemplative Prayer.* Minneapolis: Augsburg, 2003.

McGrath, Alister. *Beyond the Quiet Time: Practical Evangelical Spirituality.* Vancouver, BC, Canada: Regent College, 2003.

Merton, Thomas. *Conjectures of a Guilty Bystander.* New York: Image, 1968.

Moon, Gary W. *Falling for God: Saying Yes to His Extravagant Proposal.* Colorado Springs: WaterBrook, 2004.

Moore, Thomas. *Care of the Soul: A Guide for Cultivating Depth and Sacredness in Everyday Life.* New York: HarperCollins, 1992.

———. *Discovering Everyday Spirituality: Place.* VHS. Alexandria, VA: PBS Home Video, 2000.

Mouw, Richard J. *Praying at Burger King.* Grand Rapids: Eerdmans, 2007.

Muller, Wayne. *Sabbath: Finding Rest, Renewal, and Delight in Our Busy Lives.* New York: Bantam, 1999.

Murray, Andrew. *The Practice of God's Presence.* New Kensington, PA: Whitaker House, 1999.

Norris, Kathleen. *The Cloister Walk.* New York: Riverhead, 1996.

Nouwen, Henri J. M. *Bread for the Journey: A Daybook of Wisdom and Faith.* New York: HarperCollins, 1997.

———. *The Only Necessary Thing: Living a Prayerful Life.* New York: Crossroad, 1999.

———. *The Return of the Prodigal Son: A Story of Homecoming.* New York: Image, 1994.

O'Neill, Eugene. *Long Day's Journey into Night.* New Haven, CT: Yale University, 1956.

Orsi, Robert, ed. *Gods of the City: Religion and the American Urban Landscape.* Bloomington: Indiana University, 1999.

Pascal, Blaise. *Pensées.* Translated by A. J. Krailsheimer. Baltimore: Penguin, 1966.

PBS. "Storefront Churches." Religion and Ethics, July 14, 2006. www.pbs .org/w.net/religionandethics/week946/feature.html.

Pennington, M. Basil. *Centered Living: The Way of Centering Prayer.* Liguori, MO: Liguori/Triumph, 1999.

Phillippe, Jacques. *Time for God: A Guide to Prayer.* Boston: Pauline, 2005.

Pier, Mac, and Katie Sweeting. *The Power of a City at Prayer: What Happens When Churches Unite for Renewal.* Downers Grove, IL: InterVarsity, 2002.

Pierce, Linda Breen. *Choosing Simplicity: Real People Finding Peace and Fulfillment in a Complex World.* Carmel, CA: Gallagher, 2000.

Piper, John. *Desiring God.* Sisters, OR: Multnomah, 2003.

Rahner, Karl. *Encounters with Silence.* Westminster, MD: Newman, 1960.

Rolheiser, Ronald. *The Holy Longing: The Search for a Christian Spirituality.* New York: Doubleday, 1999.

Rosenwald, Michael S. "The Steak-Filled Room: Power-Lunch Hotspots for Cutting Deals and Trading Juicy Gossip." *Washington Post,* January 15, 2007.

Rupnik, Marko Ivan. *In the Fire of the Burning Bush: An Initiation to the Spiritual Life.* Grand Rapids: Eerdmans, 2004.

Sine, Christine. *Sacred Rhythms: Finding a Peaceful Pace in a Hectic World.* Ada, MI: Baker, 2003.

Spong, John Shelby. "The Urban Church: Symbol and Reality." *Christian Century,* September 12–19, 1984.

Spurgeon, C. H. *All of Grace.* New Kensington, PA: Whitaker House, 1981, 1983.

———. *Prayer and Spiritual Warfare.* New Kensington, PA: Whitaker House, 1998.

Steindl-Rast, David. *Gratefulness, the Heart of Prayer: An Approach to Life in Fullness.* Mahwah, NJ: Paulist, 1984.

Tanner, Kathryn, ed. *Spirit in the Cities: Searching for the Soul in the Urban Landscape.* Minneapolis: Augsburg Fortress, 2004.

Teresa of Avila. *Selections from "The Interior Castle."* New York: HarperCollins, 2004.

Teresa, Mother. *Everything Starts from Prayer: Mother Teresa's Meditations on Spiritual Life for People of All Faiths.* Edited by Anthony Stern. Ashland, OR: White Cloud, 2000.

Tozer, A. W. *The Pursuit of God.* Camp Hill, PA: WingSpread, 2006.

Underhill, Evelyn. *The Spiritual Life.* Atlanta: Ariel, 2000.

Vergara, Camilo Jose. *How the Other Half Worships.* Piscataway, NJ: Rutgers University, 2005.

Waldron, Robert. *Poetry as Prayer: The Hound of Heaven.* Boston: Pauline, 1999.

Warren, Rick. *The Purpose-Driven Life: What on Earth Am I Here For?* Grand Rapids: Zondervan, 2002.

Wesley, Charles. *Charles Wesley: A Reader.* Edited by John Tyson. Oxford, England: Oxford University, 2002.

Wilder, Thornton. *Our Town.* New York: Perennial, 2003.

Willard, Dallas. *Renovation of the Heart: Putting on the Character of Christ.* Colorado Springs: NavPress, 2002.

Wordsworth, William. "Intimations of Immortality from Recollections of Early Childhood." In *The Oxford Book of English Verse: 1250–1900.* Edited by Arthur Quiller-Couch. London: Oxford University, 1963.

Wright, Paul A. *Mother Teresa's Prescription: Finding Happiness and Peace in Service.* Notre Dame, IN: Ave Maria, 2006.

Yancey, Philip. *Finding God in Unexpected Places.* New York: Doubleday, 2005.

———. *The Jesus I Never Knew.* Grand Rapids: Zondervan, 1995.

———. *What's So Amazing About Grace?* Grand Rapids: Zondervan, 1997.

Yount, David. *Spiritual Simplicity: Simplify Your Life and Enrich Your Soul.* New York: Fireside, 1999.

You've Got Mail. DVD. Directed by Nora Ephron. Burbank, CA: Warner Bros., 1998.

Zweig, Connie. *The Holy Longing: The Hidden Power of Spiritual Yearning.* New York: Tarcher/Putnam, 2003.

INDEX

9/11 . . . . 124, 146, 190–191

Aaron (brother of Moses) 124

addiction 125, 149–150

adoration 174, 180–181, 184

agoraphobia 11

AIDS 130–131

"Amazing Grace" 148–149

Amos (prophet) 89

Angelus 113

Antioch 161, 164, 176

apartment 26, 88, 93, 95,
113–114, 119, 138

art 103–104, 106–109,
128–129

atheist 29, 68–70, 74

Autrey, Wesley 22–23

Augustine, Saint (of Hippo) . . . 4, 35

Baab, Lynne M. 80

Babylon 81

Baez, Joan 149

Bakke, Ray 163, 176–177,
179–180

Barrett, Anne 93–94

Bartimaeus 18–129

Baum, L. Frank 2

Beckett, Sister Wendy 108, 111

being, state of . . . 9–11, 13, 30–32,
35–36, 55, 57–60,
75–77, 101–102, 176

Benson, Herbert 71–72

Berlin 147

Best, Harold 105, 176, 178

Bible 2, 13, 17, 69,
96, 103, 114, 141,
144, 151, 166, 173,
179, 182, 183.
See also Scripture

New Testament 15

Old Testament 123, 163

Bill, J. Brent 11–12, 22

BlackBerry (PDA) 17, 58, 65,
71, 73

blessed 12–18, 55, 130,
145–146, 190–191

blessing 24, 100, 194

Bloom, Anthony 15–16, 35–36

Boston, Massachusetts 93, 96

breaks 29–30, 57

breath, breathing . . . 14–16, 20, 25,
        32, 54, 57, 58,
        61, 62, 82
breath prayer . . . 14–16, 20, 25, 54,
        61, 80. *See also* Jesus Prayer
Brent J. Bill. . . . . . *See* Bill, J. Brent
Brendel, Alfred. 93
Broadway 32, 92, 103, 147
Buechner, Frederick. 3, 4, 49
busyness. . . . 44–63, 49, 50, 64–65,
        67–68, 70–71, 73–74,
        75, 77, 81, 84–85.
        See also haste; Sabbath
café 48, 183, 194
Calcutta . . . . 21. *See also*
        Teresa, Mother
candles 34, 82, 114, 120,
        132, 162, 170
caritas. 122
Carmelite nuns and monks . . . .
        55–56, 75, 114
Carnegie Hall 102
Carville, James. 98
catacombs . . . 164, 170, 176–177, 180
cathedral. 3, 20, 67, 102–104,
        106, 112–113, 159, 188
Catholic. 36, 75
Celebration of Discipline 14,
        89, 124
cell phone. 17, 31, 57–58,
        64, 73, 77
Celtic. 188
centeredness 30, 36, 51,
        57–59, 145

centering-prayer 34, 52, 56, 57,
        75–76, 79, 111, 144–145
Central Park 37, 79, 109, 111
CEOs. 67, 98
chapel. 30, 36, 40, 77–78,
        114, 158–159
chaplain. 28–29, 30
charismatic 164, 172
Chartres cathedral 112–113
Chartres, France 38, 67, 184
Chicago, Illinois 109
Chicago (the musical). 32
choir 97, 149, 172
Choosing Simplicity. 95
Christ. 4, 54, 58, 70, 76,
        80, 90, 113, 123,
        141, 159, 171, 183
Christian 161, 164, 167, 170,
        179, 180
cityscape 4–5, 10, 40, 109, 189
Collins, Judy 149
community 55–56, 124,
        131–134, 156–170
Communion (Eucharist) 162
compassion 5, 13, 24, 42, 58,
        74, 123, 139–140,
        143–145, 150
Compostela, Spain. 3
Conjectures of a Guilty Bystander . . .
        10, 30
contemplation . . . 1, 26–43, 44–63,
        77–78, 104, 105, 106–
        111, 115, 118, 187
Corinth 161, 164, 182

corporate worship . . . . . *See* worship
of God; worship services
CPA (continuous partial attention) . . .
70–71
crafts. 36–37, 133–134
craftsmanship 86, 99
cross 18, 41, 80, 114
crowd-sickness. 11, 45
crowds 4, 9–25, 162–163
Dalai Lama 111
Dallas, Texas 104
Dark Ages 103
dark and light 21
David (king) 18, 50, 105, 145
Davis, Susie. 73–74, 123
Day Christ Died, The. 70
Day, Dorothy 12–13
details, finding God in 54–55
Dickinson, Emily 109–110
discipline. 13, 34, 54, 89,
144–145
Disrud, Thomas 77
diversity. . 3–4, 7, 11–12, 112–113,
159–161, 161–162,
164–166, 176–177
Dolce Vita, La. 4
Doors into Prayer 53
downtown. 25, 26, 43
Dublin, Ireland 147
Easter 26, 103, 179–180
Eastern Orthodox Christianity . . . 15,
54, 107. *See also*
Bloom, Anthony
Ebb, Fred. 21

Edwards, Tilden 78–79
Egypt 89, 158, 163, 175
elevator. 20, 25, 37, 43, 45,
46, 123, 138, 182
Elijah (prophet). 38–39
envy 12, 66–67
Episcopal 104
eternity 98, 102
Eternity (perfume) 47–48
Eucharist (Communion) 162
Ezekiel 38
Faster 45
Finding God on the A Train 182
Florence, Italy 102, 106
focus on God. . . . 1, 16–17, 31–32,
35–37, 40,52, 56–57,
59, 61, 62, 81–82,
107, 113, 151. *See also*
centeredness;
centering prayer
Foster, Richard 14, 89,
93–96, 124, 167,
174–175, 180
France. 38, 67, 112–113, 184
Francis of Assisi, Saint 22,
91–92, 115
Frost, Robert 46
freeways. 45, 144, 175
Galilee 21
Garrett, Thomas 91
Gavigan, Thomas P. 76, 87–88
Gleick, James. 45
glory of creation 63, 93, 107,
158, 168, 192

glory of God 50, 54, 90,
       105, 152, 173
God in others 11–12, 27, 102
Gods of the City 164–165
Godsickness 35–37
Gonzalez, David 160–162
gospel . . 15, 17, 18, 21, 50, 69–70,
       81, 100, 103, 105, 111,
       122, 128, 141, 143, 146,
       154, 163, 178, 179, 181
Goulart, Frances Sheridan 134
grace
    "Amazing Grace" 148–149
    of God 46–47, 53, 78–79,
       92, 95–96, 97–98, 148–149,
       155, 166, 191, 193
    mealtime prayer . . . 78, 114,120
Grand Canyon (film) 46
Grand Canyon National Park . . . . .
       92, 184
gratitude . . . 27, 32, 41, 59, 73, 80,
       97, 100, 118, 120,
       129–130, 175, 181, 184,
       186, 188–194
Griffin, Emilie 35, 52–53
Griffin, Michael 160
Gutierrez, Gustavo 144
Hamlin, Rick 68, 182
Hamma, Robert M. 110–111
Hammarskjold, Dag 94–95
happiness 3, 65–66, 76, 145
Harlem 41, 160, 164
haste 140

heart . . . 11, 13, 40, 43, 67, 89–90,
       98, 107, 115, 125, 129,
       135, 141–146, 151–153,
       154, 168, 174, 177, 193
    prayer of the heart 16, 25,
       53–54, 115, 124, 180
    restless heart 4–5, 35, 74
    solitude or silence of the heart . . .
       14, 33, 34, 37,
       81, 110–112, 114
heart attack 36, 69
heaven 2, 38, 89, 96,
       106, 110, 179
heavens, the 39, 63, 105,
       106, 107, 152, 168, 192
Hebrew
    Jews 81, 89, 158, 170, 176
    language 121
    prophets . . . 18, 21–22, 38–39,
       82, 89, 100, 123,
       126, 141, 145, 174
    Scriptures . . . 145–156, 167, 172
Helsinki, Finland 147
highway . . . . *See* freeway
HIV . . . . *See* AIDS
Hobson, Peter 173
Holy Longing, The 122, 141
home . . . 8, 32–33, 39, 48, 86–87,
       99–100, 113–115,
       117, 131–133, 148, 162
homelessness 5, 9, 13–14, 16,
       17, 24, 72–73, 119–121,
       125–128, 131, 137, 139,

142–143, 146, 149–150,
157–159, 161–162, 165,
173, 181

Hopkins, Gerard Manley. 6

Horwitz, Claudia 10, 31, 51

hospice 47–48

hospital 28–30, 46, 125,
133, 156, 182

hot line 132–133

"Hound of Heaven" 149–150

houses of worship. 3, 5, 10, 26,
81, 104, 112–113, 115,
117, 118, 126, 157, 159,
161, 163–165, 169,
171–187

How the Other Half Worships. . . 160

Hungering Dark, The. . . . . *See*
Buechner, Frederick

Hurricane Katrina. . . 124, 139, 146

hurry . . . . *See* haste

hurry-sickness 45

Hutchinson, Anne. 94, 96

Hybels, Bill 68

illness. . . . . *See* sickness

instant messaging 33, 58,
62, 71. *See also* BlackBerry

Interior Castle. 115

Intervale Jewish Community
Center 164–165

intervention 22–23, 149

Jacomo, Tommy 98

Japanese Presbyterian Church,
Seattle 165

Jeon, Arthur 66, 143

Jericho. 18, 124, 144

Jerusalem 2, 3, 7, 18, 22,
38–39, 145, 163–164,
165, 179, 181

Jesus Prayer 54, 80

Jews 12, 54, 78, 121,
164–165, 172, 179, 181.
See also Hebrew

John Paul II 111

Jordan, Vernon 97

Judaism. 12, 54, 78, 121,
164–165, 172, 179, 181.
See also Hebrew

Judeo–Christian 93, 158

Julian of Norwich, Dame 55

Katrina, hurricane. . . 124, 139, 146

Kelly, Thomas 16–17, 21,
32–33, 36, 59, 98

Kennedy Center for the
Performing Arts 104

Kew Gardens, London 109

knitting . . . . *See* crafts

Knitting Guild of America 133

knowing God 16, 40,
58–59, 71–72, 73, 79

La Dolce Vita 4

Laubach, Frank 6, 51, 75–76,
82, 84–85, 142

Lawrence, Brother. . . 55, 75–76, 84

letting go 91–92, 151

Lennon, John. 111

Levy, Steven. 71

Lewis, C. S. 53–54, 69,
                71, 73, 181, 190
Lewis, Mark. 11
Lighthouse International. . . 129–130
Linthicum, Robert C. 2
London, England. . . 103, 109, 142,
                147, 149, 152, 174, 179
Los Angeles, California. . . 4, 46, 104
Louisville, Kentucky 4, 10, 24
love 3, 10, 12, 38, 69, 77, 122,
                124, 136–127, 128–129,
                134, 144, 145, 154, 163
        for God. 35, 53, 56,
                89, 126–127, 128,
                173–174, 180
        of God. . . 12, 35, 48, 52, 53–54,
                55, 58, 72, 79, 82, 92,
                114–115, 128, 134, 141,
                150, 173, 174, 186
Lutheran 17, 78, 104, 158
luxuries 92, 95
Magnificent Defeat, The 3
Maine 77–78, 188
Making Room for God . . . . *See*
                Matthews, Melvyn
Malamud, Bernard 2
Manhattan, New York 3, 9, 29,
                37, 86, 103, 109, 140,
                146, 160, 161, 164,
                183, 184
marketplace. 2, 11, 22, 146
Markings 94–95
Martha (sister of Lazarus) 50
Mary (sister of Lazarus) 50

Mason, Kelly Murphy. . . . 190–191
Mass 103, 111, 159
Masters, Edgar Lee 69
Matthews, Melvyn 56, 59, 115
Maynell, Wilfred 149, 150
meals 55, 75, 78, 126,
                130–132, 142–143. *See also*
                Eucharist (Communion);
                grace; mealtime prayer
Meals on Wheels. 130–132
Merchant of Venice 152
mercy, of God 14, 37, 54, 111,
                138–155, 166, 178
Merry England 149–150
Merton, Thomas 10, 12, 24,
                30, 37, 111–112
Middle Ages 3, 20, 103
mind, the 3, 14, 16, 31,
                33–34, 43, 76, 85, 103
mindfulness 12–13, 17, 31,
                62, 75, 85, 97
Mind the Light 11–12
ministry. . . 119–137, 165–166, 179
        of Jesus. . . . 18, 38, 50, 89, 163
Misérables, Les 147
monastery 55–56, 75–76,
                108, 109, 125, 150
monks 55, 71, 75–76,
                84, 125, 141
Moore, Thomas 3, 39
Moses 18, 50, 124, 158, 183
Mother Teresa. . . *See* Teresa, Mother
Mouw, Richard J. 178
Moyers, Bill 108

Mozart, Wolfgang Amadeus . . . 102

Muller, Wayne 81

multitudes. . . . . *See* crowds

museums 102, 106–107, 108, 117–118

music 61, 85, 97, 102–103, 104–106, 107, 109, 161, 172, 173, 179, 181, 187

mystic 48

National Air and Space Museum 107

nature . . . . . 63, 93, 107, 109–110, 117, 158, 168, 175–176, 186. *See also* glory, of creation

Natural, The. 2

Nazareth 18, 22, 81, 89

Nehemiah. 18, 81

New Orleans. . . . 35, 124, 139, 146

Newton, John 148–149

New York City 35, 139–140, 165, 183–184, 190–191

New Yorker. 140

New York Magazine 3

New York Times 67, 160

Newsweek. 71

Nightingale, Florence 31

noise . . . . . . 26–43, 105, 171–172, 185. *See also* quietness

Norman, Jesseye 149

oases . . . . . 64, 104–105, 106–107, 109, 112–118. *See also* pauses; Sabbath; solitude

One Good Work at a Time 134

Orthodox . . . . *See* Eastern Orthodox Christianity; Jews

Our Town 101–102, 184

Palm Restaurant 97–98

parable. . . 74, 87–88, 96, 122, 125, 141, 143–144, 154–155

Paris, France. 22, 40, 109, 112, 147, 175, 182

Parker, Rebecca 79

parks . . . 37–38, 79, 101, 109–111, 116, 117, 183, 191

Paul (the apostle) 77, 164, 181–182

pauses . . . . . 16, 39, 46, 51–52, 71, 73, 75, 77–78, 80, 113, 178, 180. *See also* oases; peace; quietness; silence; Sabbath; solitude

PDA (personal digital assistant). . . . *See* BlackBerry

peace . . . . . 3, 5, 10, 13, 16, 22, 31, 34, 35–36, 37, 38, 43, 58, 59, 64, 70, 73, 79, 85, 90–91, 93–94, 101–118, 155, 166, 176, 189. *See also* oases; pauses; quietness; silence; Sabbath; solitude

Pennington, M. Basil 56–57, 144–145

Pentecost 39, 164, 167, 180, 181–182, 191

penthouse apartment 65–67

Pierce, Linda Breen 95

Pietà 102

pilgrims 2, 3, 18, 20, 111,
      113, 163–164

pine trees 77–78

Piper, John 177

Posey, Parker 45

praise 6, 12, 18, 23, 33, 41, 50,
     53, 54, 97, 98, 104,
     105, 106, 111–112, 135,
     153, 158, 172, 180, 185.
     See also worship

prayer . . . 8, 13–14, 20–22, 30, 48,
     50, 67, 71, 90–91, 125,
     136–137, 141, 143, 144,
     151, 155, 162, 166, 172,
     175, 177–178, 180–181,
     186, 193. *See also* gratitude

breath prayer 14–16, 20,
     25, 54, 61, 80

centering prayer 34, 52, 56,
     57, 75–76, 79, 111, 144–145

finding time and space for . . . .
     1–2, 16–18, 26–43, 47,
     51–54, 57–58, 61–62,
     67–68, 71–85, 90, 109–118,
     177–178, 181–184

for others (intercessory) . . . 125,
     131–132, 193–194

hesechast (ceaseless prayer) . . . .
     51, 54

in community 13–14, 162,
     166–170, 174

Jesus Prayer 54, 80

Mother Teresa and 20–21,
     33, 128

silent or quiet prayer . . . 14–17,
     24, 26, 28, 30–35, 54,
     56–57, 58–60, 61, 71–74,
     75–76, 132, 133, 161–162

"siren prayer" 28

spontaneous 13–16, 28

vespers 104, 114

work or acts of service as . . . . .
     20–21, 33, 55–56,
     123–125, 128, 131,
     133–134

Presbyterian 104, 109, 165

priest 36, 87–88, 125

prison 23, 122, 134, 147

prophets 18, 21–22, 38–39,
     82, 89, 100, 123, 126,
     141, 145, 174

Protestant 75, 78, 110, 175

Purpose–Driven Life, The 54,
     122–123

psalms 15, 34, 50, 77, 105, 142

Psychotherapy and Spirituality
 Institute 103

questions 73, 123, 151–152

quietness 10, 36–41, 46,
     171–172. *See also* oases; pauses;
    peace; silence; Sabbath; solitude

in contemplation/reflection . . .
     104, 109, 111, 118, 167,
     169, 181–184, 187

in prayer . . . 14–17, 24, 26, 28,
     30–35, 54, 56–57,

58–60, 61, 71–74, 75–
76, 132, 133, 161–162
"quiet time" with God. 30,
32, 34–35, 38, 56,
71–74, 75, 113, 180
Rachael's Women's Center. . . . .
126–127, 131
Reflecting Pool. 111
reflection 79, 94, 102, 109,
148, 151, 171–172, 180
restaurant. 64, 97–98, 139,
178, 183
resting 4–5, 10, 35, 73, 80–82,
91. *See also* Sabbath; stress
rhythms 61, 78, 81–82, 85
Rockefeller Center. 183
Rolheiser, Ronald 122, 141
Roman Catholic. . . . . . *See* Catholic
Rome. 2, 161, 164, 170,
176–177, 182
rosary 112, 181, 183
Sabbath. . . . . 76–85.
See also worship of God
Sabbath Keeping. 80
Sacks, Moishe 164–165
sacred space 102–104, 110,
112–114, 157, 169, 172,
179–180. *See also* worship
of God; houses of worship
Samaritan 125, 144, 150, 176
San Francisco, California. 146
Satan 2
Scripture 14, 18, 38–39, 49,
93, 126. *See also* Bible

Sears Tower, Chicago. 109, 184
Seattle, Washington . . . 160, 165, 184
seduction 65–66
September 11, 2001. . . . . . *See* 9/11
Sermon on the Mount 18,
146, 155
servanthood . . . . 124, 127–128.
See also service, acts of
service, acts of 119, 126–137,
141, 143, 160, 165–166,
174. *See also* servanthood
Shakespeare. 103, 152
shelters 13–14, 119–122,
126–128, 133, 142–143,
158, 161–162, 173
sickness
AIDS 130–131
Godsickness 35–37
hurry-sickness. 45
silence 21, 26–43, 77, 161,
167–168, 171–172. *See*
also oases; peace; pauses;
quietness; Sabbath;
solitude
inner silence . . . 30–39, 43, 57,
94, 111–112, 114–115
simplicity . . . 55, 86–100, 114–115
siren. 5, 26–27, 28, 31, 42,
171–172
solitude . . . . . 14, 21, 85, 156–170.
See also oases; peace;
pauses; quietness;
Sabbath; silence
Sondheim, Steven 102

sound 26–43, 105, 111, 112,
          113–114, 132, 171–172,
          175, 191. *See also*
          music; noise
space . . . 10–13, 24, 39, 56, 58–60,
          66–67, 71, 78, 80, 93,
          97–98, 99–100, 102–104,
          106, 110, 111, 112,
          113–114, 115–116,
          158–159, 169, 172,
          179–180, 183–184, 191
National Air and Space
          Museum 107
Spain 3
Spiritual Activist, The 10, 31
Spiritual Simplicity 93, 96
spontaneous prayer 13–16, 28
Spoon River Anthology . . 69, 167–168
Steindl-Rast, David 189
status 65–67, 97–98, 99,
          122–123
stillness 26–43, 71–74, 77–78,
          106–107, 114–115.
          See also oases; peace;
          pauses; quietness; silence;
          simplicity; solitude
"Stopping by Woods on a Snowy
          Evening" 46
storefront churches . . . 159–161, 164
Strawberry Fields 111
stress 2–3, 11, 64–85, 101
Sutton, Martin Hope 39–40
Talbot, John Michael 92

taxi . . . 19, 28, 45, 51, 139, 140, 181
temple 18, 38, 112,
          163–165, 172, 179
Teresa of Avila, Saint 115, 123
Teresa, Mother (of Calcutta) 6,
          20–21, 33, 128, 131
Testament of Devotion, A 16, 98
Time of Your Life, The 73
thankfulness . . . . *See* gratitute
theater 101–102, 103–104,
          147, 152
Thompson, Francis 149–150
Tokyo, Japan 147
Too Busy Not to Pray 68
transcendent moments . . 10, 46, 97
Transfiguration 50, 179
Trevi Fountain, Rome 182
Tubman, Harriet 31, 91
tzedakah 121
Unceasing Worship 105, 176
Underhill, Evelyn 35, 37
United Parcel Service (UPS) 27
unlovable people 128–129
urban burnout 3
Urban Christian, The 163,
          177, 179
Valjean, Jean 147
Vatican City 4
vespers 104, 114
Voice in the City, A 173
voluntary simplicity 91–92,
          95–96. *See also* simplicity
volunteer . . . . *See* service, acts of

Walden Pond 97
Waldron, Robert 150
Warren, Rick 54, 122–123, 166
Washington DC 22, 87, 98,
        104, 107, 111, 119, 126,
        130, 139, 143, 158, 161
Wesley, John 123, 174
white noise 27
Willard, Dallas 90, 165–166
Wizard of Oz, The 2
Wordsworth, William 48
World Trade Center 124,
        146, 190–191
worship of God . . . 5, 8, 16, 18, 34,
        41, 59, 61, 78, 80, 81, 105,
        106, 117, 161, 165–166,
        170, 171–187. *See also*
        houses of worship
worship services (corporate
    worship) 9, 50, 61, 79–80,
        158, 160, 163–164, 167,
        169–170, 171–187.
        See also music; Sabbath
Wright, Paul A. 3
Yamanouchi, Tayeko 34
Yount, David 93, 96–97
You've Got Mail 45

About the Author

MARCY HEIDISH has lived in cities most of her life. She is the award-winning author of eight previous books, many of which have spiritual themes. One of these is *A Woman Called Moses,* which was made into a television movie starring Cicely Tyson. Heidish, an Edgar Award nominee, is the recipient of a National Endowment for the Arts grant. She has been an active volunteer with homeless women, a hot line, and the Lighthouse for the Blind.

To learn more about WaterBrook Press and view our catalog of products, log on to our Web site:

www.waterbrookpress.com

WATERBROOK
PRESS